Housing and Inclusive Growth

OECD

This work is published under the responsibility of the Secretary-General of the OECD. The opinions expressed and arguments employed herein do not necessarily reflect the official views of OECD member countries.

This document, as well as any data and map included herein, are without prejudice to the status of or sovereignty over any territory, to the delimitation of international frontiers and boundaries and to the name of any territory, city or area.

The statistical data for Israel are supplied by and under the responsibility of the relevant Israeli authorities. The use of such data by the OECD is without prejudice to the status of the Golan Heights, East Jerusalem and Israeli settlements in the West Bank under the terms of international law.

Note by Turkey
The information in this document with reference to "Cyprus" relates to the southern part of the Island. There is no single authority representing both Turkish and Greek Cypriot people on the Island. Turkey recognises the Turkish Republic of Northern Cyprus (TRNC). Until a lasting and equitable solution is found within the context of the United Nations, Turkey shall preserve its position concerning the "Cyprus issue".

Note by all the European Union Member States of the OECD and the European Union
The Republic of Cyprus is recognised by all members of the United Nations with the exception of Turkey. The information in this document relates to the area under the effective control of the Government of the Republic of Cyprus.

Please cite this publication as:
OECD (2020), *Housing and Inclusive Growth*, OECD Publishing, Paris, *https://doi.org/10.1787/6ef36f4b-en*.

ISBN 978-92-64-95213-3 (print)
ISBN 978-92-64-36281-9 (pdf)

Foreword

This report brings together two strands of work at the OECD: inequality and inclusive growth, on the one hand, and housing policies on the other.

Over the past three decades, the OECD has documented trends in inequality, examined its drivers, and assessed the effectiveness of a range of policies to tackle poverty and promote more inclusive growth. In so doing, the OECD has put inequality and inclusive growth at the core of international agendas, including the G7 and G20, with publications such as *Divided We Stand: Why Inequality Keeps Rising, Under Pressure: The Squeezed Middle Class,* and the *OECD Framework for Policy Action on Inclusive Growth.* This report extends this analysis by focusing on housing and the ways in which it matters for inclusive growth.

At the same time, this report contributes to a broader OECD-wide project on housing. The OECD Housing Project, led by the Economic Policy Committee (EPC), draws on the expertise and contributions from numerous committees, including the Employment, Labour and Social Affairs Committee (ELSAC); the Environment Policy Committee (EPOC); the Regional Development Policy Committee (RDPC); the Committee on Statistics and Statistical Policy (CSSP); and, the Committee on Fiscal Affairs (CFA), among others. This report supports the development of an integrated housing policy approach and a strategic vision for implementation.

This report was written under the overall supervision of the OECD Secretary-General, Angel Gurría, and the Special Counsellor to the Secretary-General, Gabriela Ramos. It was produced by the Directorate of Employment, Labour and Social Affairs, under the leadership of Stefano Scarpetta. Willem Adema supervised the preparation of this report, within the Social Policy Division led by Monika Queisser. Willem Adema and Marissa Plouin drafted the report, and Pauline Fron and Salomé Bakaloglou provided statistical and research assistance. Several aspects of the analysis draw on the analytical work of Horacio Levy on household consumption estimates, prepared for *Under Pressure: The Squeezed Middle Class.* We gratefully acknowledge the suggestions provided or channelled by delegates of the Employment, Labour and Social Affairs Committee and the Working Party on Social Policy. We would also like to thank colleagues from across the OECD who provided valuable comments throughout the development of the report, including Stefano Scarpetta, Mark Pearson, Monika Queisser, Chris Clarke, Sebastian Königs, Sarah Kups and Valerie Frey from the Directorate of Employment, Labour and Social Affairs; Romina Boarini, Ziga Zarnic and Grainne Dirwan from the Inclusive Growth Unit in the Office of the Secretary-General; Christophe André, Orsetta Causa, Boris Cournède and Peter Hoeller from the Economics Department; Bert Brys, Bethany Millar-Powell and Pierce O'Reilly from the Centre for Tax Policy; Abel Schumann from the Centre for Entrepreneurship, SMEs, Regions and Cities; and Francette Koechlin and Carlotta Balestra from the Statistics Directorate. Fatima Perez supported the preparation of this report, and Liv Gudmundson prepared it for publication.

We gratefully acknowledge the financial support of the Ford Foundation.

Table of contents

Foreword   3

Executive summary   6

1 Overview and key messages   8
  1.1. Housing is a key determinant of inclusive growth   9
  1.2. Who is at risk of housing exclusion?   11
  1.3. How can public policies foster inclusive growth?   13
  References   17
  Notes   19

2 Is the housing market an obstacle to inclusive growth? For whom?   20
  2.1. Overall trends in the housing market   21
  2.2. Good quality affordable housing is out of reach for many low-income households   24
  2.3. Many children face poor quality housing and housing instability   31
  2.4. Youth struggle to access quality, affordable housing of their own, risking a deepening of
  inter- and intra-generational inequality   34
  2.5. The vulnerable elderly face exclusion as populations age and housing prices rise   38
  2.6. The homeless population in some OECD countries is growing and increasingly diverse   41
  References   43
  Notes   48

3 How can housing policies and governance help deliver inclusive growth?   51
  3.1. Rethinking housing policies and governance to deliver Inclusive growth   52
  3.2. Overcoming the specific housing barriers facing low-income households, children, youth
  and seniors   66
  3.3. Addressing housing vulnerability to address housing vulnerability prompted by the
  COVID-19 pandemic   70
  References   71
  Notes   76

Annex A. Household consumption expenditure and measurement data   78

Annex B. Housing overburden rates, by age   79

Annex C. Trends in overall investment in housing   80

Tables

Table 2.1. Indicators of housing quality and affordability 24
Table 3.1. Housing policy considerations for more inclusive growth 53
Table 3.2. The lead housing ministry varies considerably across countries 54
Table 3.3. Types of rent control regulations, as well as their advantages and disadvantages 64
Table 3.4. Many countries introduced emergency housing measures in response to COVID-19 70

Table B.1. Housing overburden rates, by age 79
Table C.1. Overall investment in housing, 2000-19 80

Figures

Figure 1.1. Housing is the biggest household spending item, and its share has grown 10
Figure 1.2. Real-estate wealth is more evenly distributed than financial wealth 11
Figure 1.3. Children in low-income households are more likely to live in overcrowded households 12
Figure 1.4. Public investment in dwellings has fallen, while spending on housing allowances is holding up 14
Figure 1.5. The majority of countries have housing allowances, social housing and financial support for home ownership 15
Figure 2.1. In most OECD countries, owning a home is much more common than renting 22
Figure 2.2. House prices increased in many OECD countries between 2005 and 2018 23
Figure 2.3. Low-income households face a significant housing cost burden 25
Figure 2.4. The share of housing spending has increased the most for low-income households 26
Figure 2.5. Overcrowding is more prevalent among low-income households relative to other income groups 27
Figure 2.6. Housing is the biggest source of wealth for low-wealth households – as well as their biggest financial liability 30
Figure 2.7. Property liabilities make up the largest share of household debt in most OECD countries 30
Figure 2.8. Children in low-income households are more likely to be exposed to poor housing quality than children in higher-income households 33
Figure 2.9. Today's families must pay considerably more to buy a flat than previous generations. 34
Figure 2.10. In many OECD countries, youth most commonly live with their parents 36
Figure 2.11. Housing is a top concern for younger generations 37
Figure 2.12. Seniors are most likely to live in dwellings they own outright 40
Figure 3.1. Public investment in dwellings has fallen, while spending on housing allowances is holding up 55
Figure 3.2. The majority of countries have housing allowances, social housing and financial support for home ownership. 59

Boxes

Box 2.1. Basic indicators of housing quality and affordability 24
Box 2.2. Housing and health 27
Box 3.1. Social housing can be a key part of the affordable housing solution. 57
Box 3.2. Summary of country responses to the 2019 OECD Questionnaire on Affordable and Social Housing (QuASH) 59
Box 3.3. Should public policies give preference to home ownership? 61
Box 3.4. Housing and residential mobility 62
Box 3.5. Rethinking rent controls 64

Executive summary

This report explores the ways in which housing matters for inclusive growth. Drawing on the *OECD Framework for Policy Action on Inclusive Growth*, which calls on governments to invest in people and places that have been left behind, this report focuses on housing outcomes and trends, identifies groups that are at risk of housing exclusion, and points to housing policy avenues that support growth in an inclusive manner.

Housing is key to inclusive growth. It is the biggest spending item of households, and its share in household consumption has been growing over the past two decades, not just for low-income households but also for the middle class. High housing costs, and especially rising rents, have reinforced inequality between households who rent and those who own their home outright. Housing is also the main driver of wealth accumulation and biggest source of debt among most households. On a broader scale, housing and the neighbourhood in which people live have important implications for individual health, employment and educational outcomes – effects that can begin in childhood and last a lifetime.

The housing market can be a barrier to inclusive growth for some groups, such as low-income households, children, youth, seniors and the homeless. Compared to other income groups, low-income households spend a larger share of their household budget on housing, record the highest rates of overcrowding, and, over the past two decades, have experienced the biggest increase in housing spending as a share of their household budget. This means they have fewer means to invest in other areas of life that could improve their life chances and overall well-being. Children are among those most likely to live in poor quality housing and neighbourhoods, making it hard to ensure a good start in life. Today's youth are, on average, most commonly living with their parents as they face limited opportunities in the housing market. For the roughly one-third of seniors who do not own their homes outright, more than one out of ten pay over 40% of their income on housing. In addition, the current housing stock is ill equipped to support the evolving needs of a rapidly ageing population. The rate of homelessness – the homeless are by definition excluded from the housing market, has increased in a third of OECD countries. While cross-national data are hard to come by, several countries report a worrying rise in homelessness among youth, families with children, and seniors.

The COVID-19 pandemic, which continues to unfold at the time of publishing this report, has highlighted just how important housing issues are to people. Across countries, governments have introduced emergency housing policy measures to address immediate challenges, such as temporary suspensions of evictions, foreclosures or rent increases, or emergency housing solutions for the homeless. However, the pandemic has also underscored the need for governments to develop more structural responses to deal with the persistent housing challenges that the most vulnerable households face.

To that end, this report assesses the key underlying pre-COVID-19 housing policy issues and proposes a series of recommendations to support more inclusive housing outcomes. These include, on the one hand, measures to address some of the structural barriers to inclusive growth in the housing market. These include expanding the affordable housing supply, investing in improvements to housing and neighbourhoods, and making the private rental market fairer and more affordable to vulnerable tenants. A second set of proposed recommendations aims to overcome the specific housing challenges facing vulnerable groups. Measures include better targeting of public support for low-income households and the homeless, helping youth and families get on the housing ladder, and supporting the vulnerable elderly to meet their evolving housing needs.

1 Overview and key messages

This section provides an overview of the main findings in this report. It begins by outlining why housing matters for inclusive growth. It identifies groups that are at risk of housing exclusion, with a closer look at housing outcomes and opportunities among low-income households, children, youth, seniors and the homeless. Finally, it assesses how public policies can facilitate inclusive growth, with a series of recommendations to guide policy makers towards more inclusive housing outcomes.

1.1. Housing is a key determinant of inclusive growth

There is a complex relationship between housing and inequality. Housing can both reflect and reinforce inequalities across socio-economic groups, across generations, and across space. Moreover, housing policy is an important lever to support vulnerable groups and foster more inclusive economic growth – that is, growth that is distributed fairly across society and creates opportunities for all (OECD, 2015[1]). The *OECD Framework for Policy Action on Inclusive Growth* (OECD, 2018[2]) identifies housing as a key dimension of inequality and inclusion.

Housing matters for inclusive growth for several reasons. First, the large and growing weight of housing spending in household budgets affects households' ability to spend or invest in other areas that can improve individual life chances, such as education or health. Housing is on average, the single-largest expenditure of households in the OECD across all income groups (Figure 1.1 – Panel A), and people are spending more on housing than they used to (Figure 1.1 – Panel B). Consumption estimates suggest that, on average across 20 OECD countries, the share of total housing spending in household budgets rose by nearly 5 percentage points between 2005 and 2015. Over the past decade, the share of household budgets also increased for other key consumption items such as transport, health and education, yet to a much lesser extent. Going back even further in time (1995-2015), albeit for a smaller subset of countries, the share of household spending on housing increased even further.

Rising housing prices – especially for renters – are part of the reason that households are spending more on housing. On average, real house prices increased in 31 OECD countries between 2005 and 2019, with Colombia, Canada, Sweden and Israel recording the largest increases (over 80%) over this period. Meanwhile, rent prices increased over this period in all but two OECD countries, more than doubling in Turkey, Lithuania, Iceland and Estonia.

Second, housing – specifically home ownership – has important implications for wealth building and wealth inequality. Housing is, for many homeowners, the most important asset they own. Housing tend to make up around half of total assets, on average, among households, subject to cross-national differences. Home ownership can help low- and middle-income households generate wealth. Housing wealth is generally distributed more equally than other types of assets, including financial assets (Figure 1.2), resulting in lower levels of wealth inequality among countries with higher levels of home ownership (Balestra and Tonkin, 2018[3]; Causa and Woloszko, 2019[4]).[1] Housing represents a much larger source of wealth among middle-class households than among the richest households (OECD, 2019[5]).

Figure 1.1. Housing is the biggest household spending item, and its share has grown

Panel A. Household budget share by consumption item, by income class, OECD average, 2016 or latest year available

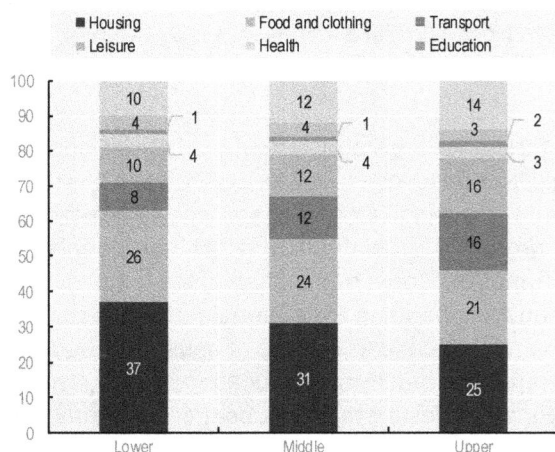

Panel B. Percentage point change in shares by item of household budgets for all income groups, OECD average, 1995-2015 and 2005-15.

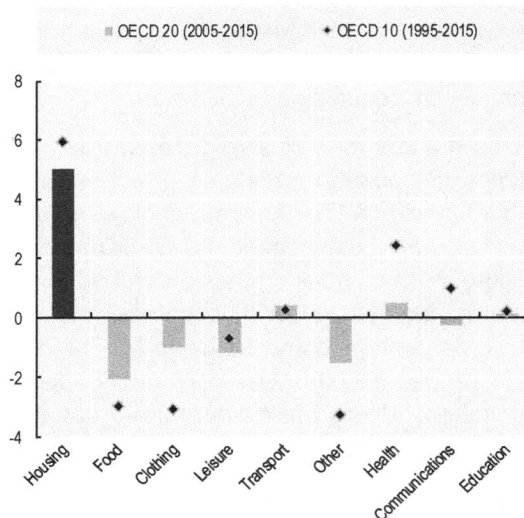

Note: Panel A: "Lower" refers to the bottom income quintile; "upper" refers to the top quintile. Panel B: OECD 20 unweighted average refers to Austria, Belgium, the Czech Republic, Finland, Germany, Greece, Hungary, Ireland, Lithuania, Luxembourg, Latvia, the Netherlands, Norway, Poland, Portugal, the Slovak Republic, Slovenia, Spain, Sweden and Turkey. OECD 10 unweighted average refers to Austria, Belgium, Finland, Germany, Greece, Ireland, Luxembourg, the Netherlands, Portugal and Sweden.

Source: (OECD, 2019[5]). Estimates based on microdata from the Eurostat Household Budget Surveys (EU HBS) 2010 and tabulations from the EU HBS 2015 for European countries, except France (Enquête Budget de Famille 2011), Spain (Encuesta de Presupuestos Familiares 2015) and the United Kingdom (Food and Living Conditions Survey 2014). Estimates draw on Pesquisa de Orçamentos Familiares 2009 for Brazil, VIII Encuesta de Presupuestos Familiares 2017 for Chile, Encuesta Nacional de Ingresos y Gastos de los Hogares 2016 for Mexico, Income and Expenditure Survey 2011 for South Africa, and Consumer Expenditure Surveys 2016 for the United States.

Third, housing can also facilitate (or impede) households' ability to move homes and thus enable workers to best match their skills to available job opportunities and improve their economic situation. Housing type and tenure matter, as do other aspects of the housing market, such as large regional housing price differences that make it more costly for households to move. Obstacles to residential mobility, in turn, affect labour mobility by creating inefficiencies in the labour market that impede workers from relocating to a job that best matches their skills (OECD, 2011[6]; Sánchez and Andrews, 2011[7]; 2011[8]; Oswald, 2009[9]; Causa and Pichelmann, Forthcoming 2020[10]).

At the same time, the debt leveraged to acquire a home also represents a liability and can expose households – and the economy more broadly – to financial risks. Indeed, among households that hold mortgage debt, property liabilities make up more than 80% of household debt across the OECD, and the largest share of debt among young households and those in the bottom and middle quintiles (Balestra and Tonkin, 2018[3]; Causa and Woloszko, 2019[4]). High levels of mortgage debt can put households at risk of bankruptcy if circumstances change. For instance, with the Global Financial Crisis millions of homeowners across the OECD went through a foreclosure, surrendered their home to a lender or sold their home via a distress sale. And while it is too soon to tell, the COVID-19 pandemic, with its large-scale effects on household incomes, may have lasting implications for housing outcomes and opportunities, once the temporary emergency measures to provide support to households struggling to cover rent, mortgage or utility payments due to a job or wage loss have been phased out (OECD, 2020[11]). Preliminary evidence from the United Kingdom and the United States suggests that renters are especially vulnerable to the economic fallout, which could lead to higher rates of evictions and homelessness.

Figure 1.2. Real-estate wealth is more evenly distributed than financial wealth

Distribution of financial and non-financial assets for households belonging to different quintiles of the wealth distribution, OECD 28 average, 2015 or latest available year

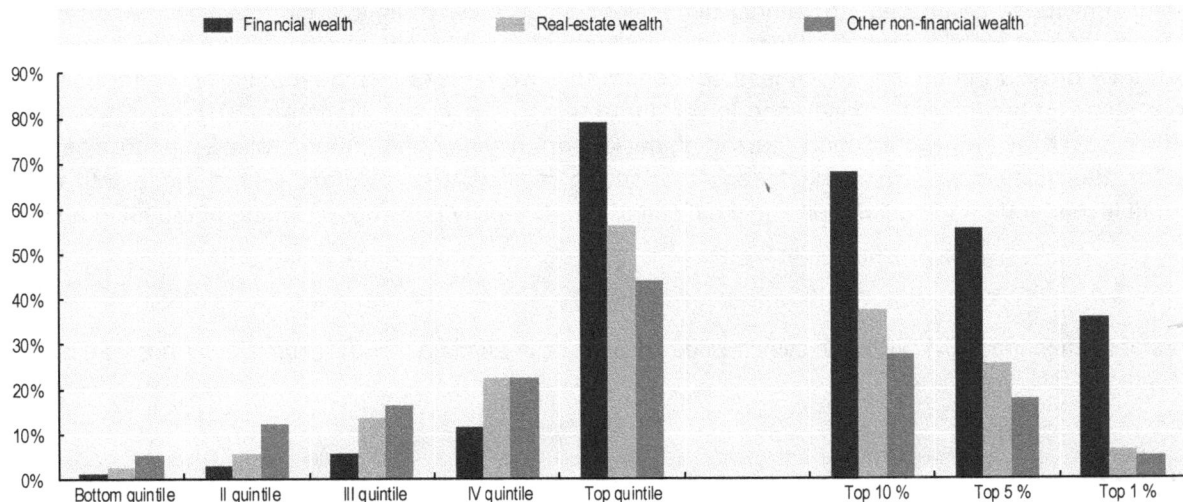

Source: (Balestra and Tonkin, 2018[3]). Based on data from the OECD Wealth Distribution database (oe.cd/wealth).

Finally, the quality of housing and the neighbourhood in which people live affects other dimensions of equality of opportunity, including health outcomes and education and employment opportunities. People living in poor quality housing and neighbourhoods tend to have worse health outcomes. Meanwhile, the *absence* of a home has an enormous impact on individual health outcomes, with the homeless dying about 30 years earlier than the general population on average (OECD, 2020[12]). Against a backdrop of high and rising levels of segregation and spatial inequality in many OECD countries (van Ham et al., 2016[13]; Massey, Rothwell and Domina, 2009[14]), residential segregation can affect residents' access to education and employment opportunities. Segregation by income levels tends to be higher in bigger, richer and more productive metropolitan areas, with the availability, quality and affordability of public transport in neighbourhoods playing an important role in connecting residents to jobs (OECD, 2018[15]).

1.2. Who is at risk of housing exclusion?

The housing market is, for some groups, a barrier to inclusive growth. For low-income households, children, youth, seniors and the homeless, reduced housing opportunities and poor housing outcomes frequently deepen inequalities.

Across the OECD, low-income households spend the biggest share of their budget on housing and, on average, live in dwellings of poorer quality. Whereas housing costs comprise a quarter of budgets of households in the upper quintile of the income distribution, it consumes, on average, well over a third of budgets of the poorest 20% of households. The high housing outlays reduce the capacity of low-income households to spend or invest in other areas that matter for inclusive growth, such as education or health. In addition, low-income households are more likely to live in overcrowded conditions[2] relative to those with higher incomes, which can generate adverse health effects. In Mexico, Poland, Latvia and the

Slovak Republic, more than 30% of low-income households are overcrowded. Housing also constitutes the biggest source of wealth and financial liabilities among low-wealth households – making home ownership both a vehicle to build wealth, as well as a potential and important source of financial risk.

Quality housing and neighbourhoods help children get a good start in life, but children are among those most likely to live in poor quality dwellings. On average, more than 1 in 5 children between 0-17 years old live in an overcrowded household in European OECD countries (Figure 1.3). Poor housing quality is a critical dimension of child poverty and represents one of the most common forms of material deprivation among children, compared to other dimensions, such as nutrition or clothing. Research on intergenerational mobility from the United States finds that low-income children are most likely to succeed when they grow up in counties with less concentrated poverty, less income inequality, better schools, a larger share of two-parent families and lower crime rates (Chetty and Hendren, 2018[16]). Children who spend more of their early childhood years in higher-opportunity neighbourhoods[3] also earn more as adults. Further, the rising cost of housing means that young families with children – even those with median income levels – are finding it increasingly difficult to afford quality housing, including purchasing a home.

Figure 1.3. Children in low-income households are more likely to live in overcrowded households

Share of children (aged 0-17) living in overcrowded households in European OECD countries, by income group, percentages, 2017

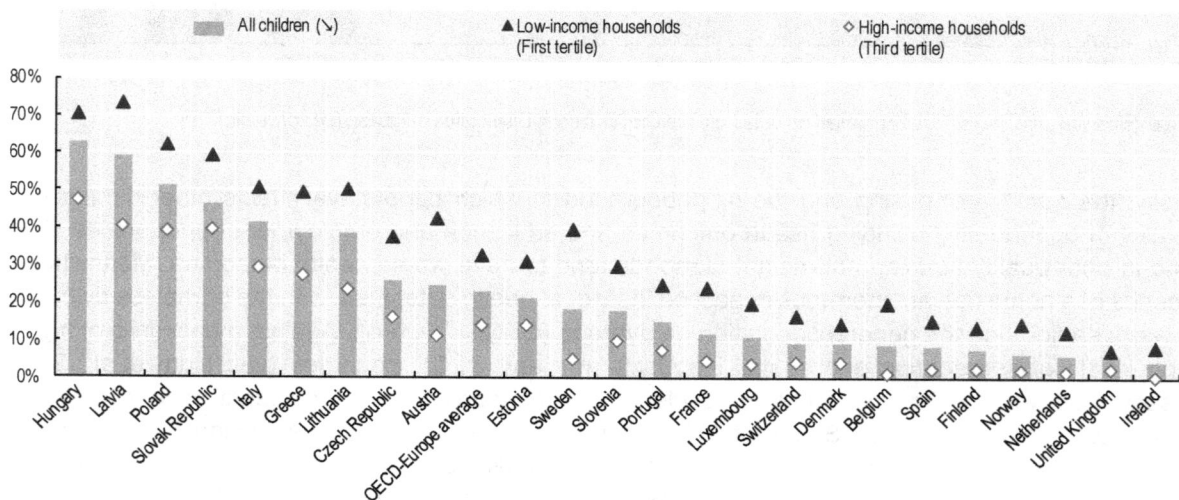

Note: 1. No information for Australia, Chile, Germany, Israel, Japan, Korea, Mexico, New Zealand, Turkey and United States due to data limitations. 2. Data for Switzerland refer to 2016. 3. The definition of overcrowding is based the EU-agreed definition (Eurostat, 2018[17]), which considers the number of rooms per household member, taking into account different factors of household composition. For a full explanation, see: www.oecd.org/els/family/HC2-1-Living-space.pdf.
Source: (OECD, 2019[18]). OECD Secretariat calculations based on the European Union Statistics on Income and Living Conditions (EU-SILC) survey, see OECD Child Well-Being Data Portal under www.oecd.org/els/family/child-well-being/data.

Opportunities in the housing market for today's youth are narrower than those of previous generations, threatening to deepen inter- and intra-generational inequality. In a context of rising rents and house prices, young adults aged 20-29 (e.g. those out of upper secondary schooling) are, on average across the OECD, most commonly living with their parents, with the biggest shares recorded in Italy (75% in 2017), the Slovak Republic (74%) and Greece (74%). In some countries, young households are finding home ownership increasingly out of reach. In the United Kingdom, home ownership rates among youth have dropped overall, and most significantly for those in the middle-income bracket (Cribb, Hood and Hoyle,

2018[19]). Relative to their peers in the past, younger people accumulate wealth less quickly, which may result from the rising age at labour market entry, less stable labour market prospects and slower earnings growth in the aftermath of the economic crisis (Clarke, Fernandez and Königs, forthcoming[20]). There is also a growing gap in some countries in access to home ownership between higher-income youth who can reply on financial support from their families and low-income youth who cannot draw on such resources: in France, nearly one-third of low-income young households were homeowners in 1973, compared to just 16% four decades later (Bonnet, Garbinti and Grobon, 2019[21]).

While the vast majority of seniors in the OECD live in homes that are owned outright, those who do not are vulnerable to increases in housing prices, as most live on fixed incomes. Housing is, for many seniors in the OECD, a source of economic stability and an important asset in old age – yet for the more than a third of seniors in the OECD who do not own their home outright, housing can represent a major source of vulnerability in old age. On average, more than one in ten seniors who do not live in homes that are owned outright are spending over 40% of their disposable income on housing costs; the share increases to around one in five non-homeowner seniors in Australia, Belgium, Chile, Greece, Japan, Sweden and the United States. Further, as they age and their physical needs evolve, low-income seniors are least likely to be able to afford improvements to their homes or to transition to a more suitable living arrangement.

Homelessness, as the most extreme form of housing exclusion, has increased in a third of OECD countries in recent years. While data on homelessness are hard to come by and compare across countries, the homeless population is estimated to be at least 1.9 million people in the 35 countries for which data are available (OECD, 2019[22]). In many OECD countries, homelessness is concentrated in big cities. For instance, Dublin accounted for around 66% of the national homeless population in Ireland in 2019, even though it only represents about a quarter of the country's total population. Homelessness is nevertheless a difficult circumstance to measure, because people experience homelessness in different ways, from the "chronically" to the "temporarily" homeless, who may be more or less visible in official statistics. In some countries, homelessness is on the rise among families with children, youth and seniors – groups who are experiencing heightened housing vulnerability (OECD, 2020[12]). For While the drivers of homelessness are multiple and complex, resulting from structural factors, institutional and systemic failures, research has identified a correlation between homelessness and rising housing costs, as well as increasing rates of poverty and evictions.

1.3. How can public policies foster inclusive growth?

The housing policy response in OECD countries could be improved to help deliver inclusive growth. As outlined in the *OECD Framework for Policy Action on Inclusive Growth,* which was designed to help governments ensure a more equitable distribution of the benefits from economic growth, housing is central to investing in people and places that have been left behind (OECD, 2018[2]).

One major housing policy challenge is that governments are, on average, investing less in the development of the housing supply than they used to. Since 2000, overall investment in housing (including both public and private) has been uneven across the OECD, while public investment in dwellings has declined sharply across the OECD on average since the Global Financial crisis (Figure 1.4). A number of factors have constrained the development of the housing supply, such as increasing construction costs, labour shortages, high land prices and/or land scarcity, or overly restrictive land regulations and planning processes. Housing supply has failed to keep pace with demand, which, in turn, has put pressure on housing affordability and created additional barriers for some groups to access quality housing.

Current design of housing support and governance in many OECD countries does not always support inclusive growth objectives. Many OECD governments have identified boosting housing affordability and stimulating the overall supply of affordable housing as a top housing policy objective. Housing support for low-income households is widespread in most countries (commonly via housing allowances and the provision of social housing), as are different types of support for homeowners and home buyers (Figure 1.5). In many countries, housing taxation in particular is one of the more powerful policy tools, and tends to generate (much) larger benefits to owner-occupied housing relative to rental housing. While home ownership has been associated with many positive spillovers, public support for home ownership, depending on the policy design, may undermine affordability and inclusion objectives in some cases. Further, the governance of housing in OECD countries, whereby it is common for different ministries and levels of government to oversee diverse aspects of housing policy, can also pose an obstacle to inclusion, making it more likely that some people fall through the cracks of public support.

Figure 1.4. Public investment in dwellings has fallen, while spending on housing allowances is holding up

Public capital transfers and public direct investment in housing development, and public spending on housing allowances and rent subsidies, OECD-25 average, as percentage GDP, 2001 to 2018

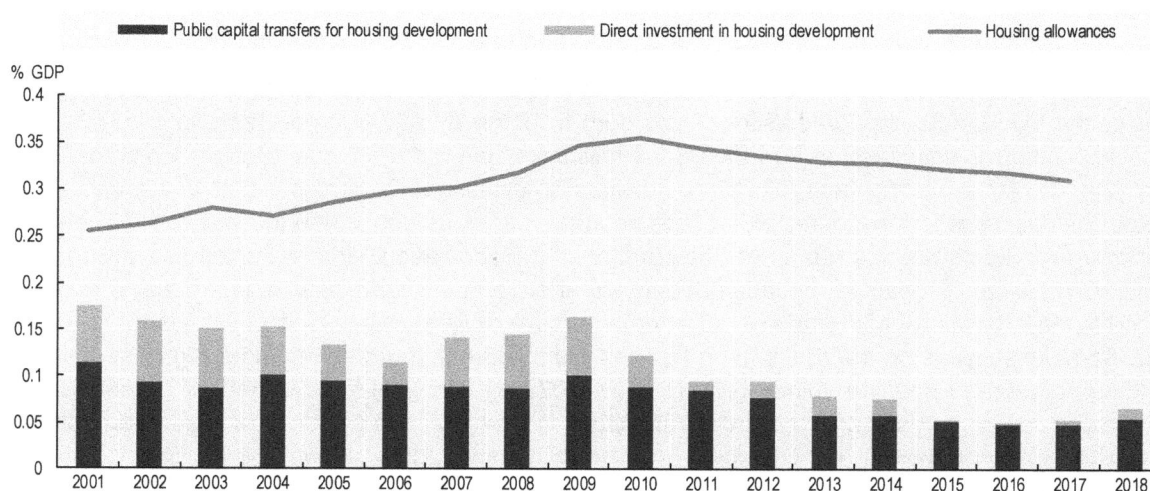

Note: The OECD-25 average is the unweighted average across the 25 OECD countries with capital transfer and gross capital formation data available for all years between 2001 and 2018. It excludes Australia, Canada, Chile, Iceland, Israel, Japan, Korea, the Netherlands, New Zealand, Turkey and the United States. Direct investment in housing development (COFOG series P5_K2CG) refers to government gross capital formation in housing development. Public capital transfers for housing development (COFOG series D9CG) refers to indirect capital expenditure made through transfers to organisations outside of government. Housing development includes, among other things, the acquisition of land needed for the construction of dwellings, the construction or purchase and remodelling of dwelling units for the general public or for people with special needs, and grants or loans to support the expansion, improvement or maintenance of the housing stock. See the Eurostat Manual on sources and methods for the compilation of COFOG Statistics (https://ec.europa.eu/eurostat/documents/3859598/5917333/KS-RA-11-013-EN.PDF) for more detail. Spending on housing allowances does not include spending on mortgage relief, capital subsidies towards construction and implicit subsidies towards accommodation costs.

Source: OECD Affordable Housing Database (http://oe.cd/ahd), Indicator PH1.1, drawing on data from the OECD National Accounts Database, www.oecd.org/sdd/na/ and provisional data from the OECD Social Expenditure Database, www.oecd.org/social/expenditure.htm.

Figure 1.5. The majority of countries have housing allowances, social housing and financial support for home ownership

Overview of housing policy instruments prior to COVID-19: Number of reporting countries adopting each policy type

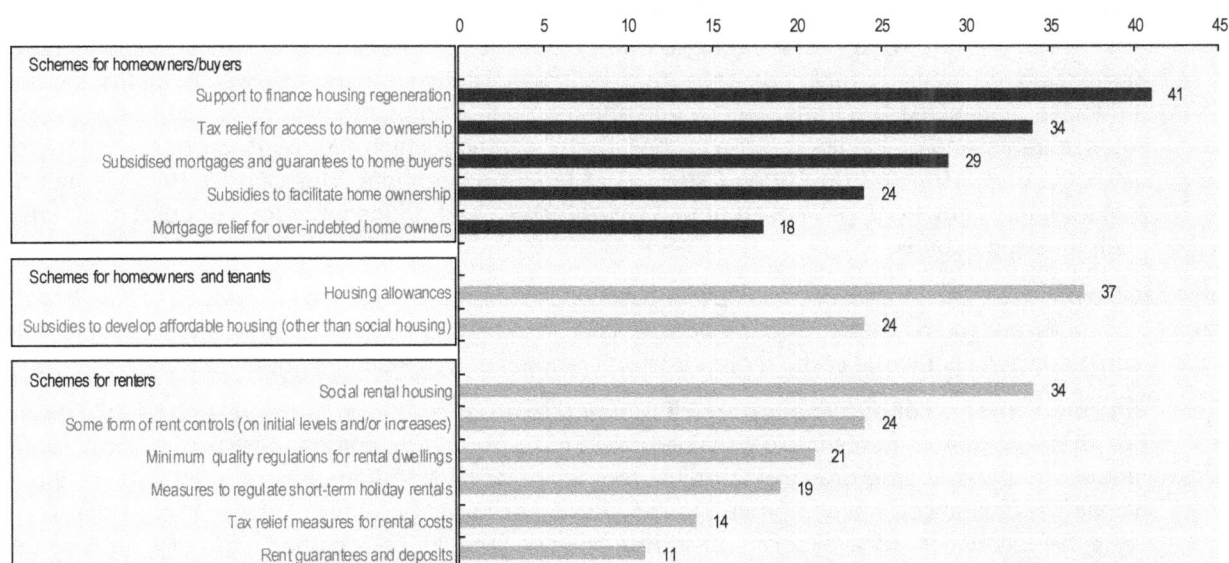

Note: 1. The list of policy types refers to those surveyed through the 2019 and 2016 Questionnaire on Affordable and Social Housing (QuASH), which gathered information from up to 49 countries; not all countries responded to all sections of the QuASH. 2. Limited information was provided for Croatia, Cyprus, Greece, Hungary, Korea, Romania, Slovenia, South Africa and Turkey.
Source: OECD Affordable Housing Database (http://oe.cd/ahd), Indicator PH1.1. Based on country responses to the 2019 and 2016 OECD QuASH.

How, then, can housing policies and governance promote inclusive growth? A first set of considerations proposes to *rethink housing policies and governance to deliver inclusive growth*. These recommendations focus on how to overcome some of the more structural barriers to inclusive growth in the housing market.

- *Make housing an integral part of an inclusive growth strategy*: Housing policies should be considered central to governments' efforts to invest in people and places that have been left behind. In light of the fragmentation of different aspects of housing policy across ministries and levels of government (e.g. housing taxation, housing support to needy households, local development decisions and land-use planning), a whole-of-government approach to housing policy is needed to achieve inclusive growth objectives. In addition, housing policies should be better coordinated with other key policy domains and services, such as health and transport, to ensure that vulnerable groups do not fall through the cracks of social support systems.

- *Expand the supply of affordable housing so that more people can access good quality dwellings*: This includes reforms to local planning, land-use and zoning regulations; a review of fiscal frameworks that may influence housing and urban development decisions; direct investments in social and affordable housing development; subsidies and other supply-side support to affordable housing developers; and advances in housing construction and building processes to drive down costs.

- *Apply an inclusive lens to the overall housing policy approach*: Considerations may include phasing out some of the (in some countries, significant) tax advantages that favour home ownership and typically benefit higher-income households, which can also hamper the pursuit of other key policy objectives to promote inclusive growth, such as related to labour mobility.

- *Improve housing and neighbourhood quality to boost individuals' access to opportunity*: Governments can provide financial support to individual households and/or landlords (in the case of rental housing) to improve housing quality; and invest in urban renewal strategies, while prioritising access to jobs, health and social services.

- *Make the private rental market more affordable*: This means striking a better balance in tenancy regulations in the private rental market between landlord and tenant rights, which could include: introducing controls of rent increases (e.g. rent stabilisation measures) within and/or across tenancies; and increasing transparency and enforcement of rental regulations to address problems when tenants and/or landlords breach their rental contact, which facilitates greater security for landlords and increased quality and security of tenure for tenants. The COVID-19 crisis has hit renters particularly hard, prompting many governments to introduce temporary support measures, such as eviction bans.

A second set of considerations focuses on how to *overcome the specific housing challenges of low-income households, children, youth, seniors and the homeless*. These measures, which target specific vulnerable groups, could complement some of the more structural recommendations highlighted above.

- *Improve targeting of public support for housing to ensure it benefits those who need it most*: For instance, governments could consider introducing more regular means-testing of social rental tenants (not just at time of entry) to adjust rent levels of better-off tenants or to incentivise those whose circumstances have improved to move to other forms of tenure. However, considerations on a fair allocation of available subsidized housing should be weighed carefully against the downsides of reduced social mixing in social housing, including the potential to exacerbate the spatial concentration of vulnerable groups, as well as challenges to the financial sustainability of the social housing system.

- *Invest in homelessness prevention and provide targeted support to the homeless*: Beyond broader investments in affordable housing that can help prevent homelessness, support should be tailored to meet the diverse needs of the homeless. Homelessness strategies should be developed with broad-based support among authorities at different levels of government as well as non-governmental actors. Governments should continue to improve data collection efforts to better understand the diverse challenges and needs of the homeless.

- *Help youth and families with children get on a stable, affordable housing ladder*: To improve youth's access to home ownership, governments may consider refining existing first-time homeowner programmes to better target (young) households in greatest need; exploring different home ownership models, including shared equity and shared ownership models; and developing programmes to enable workers on temporary/non-traditional employment contracts to be eligible to apply for a mortgage. Beyond home ownership, governments could also develop or expand supports for young people in the private rental market, social housing and co-operative living arrangements to help youth get on a stable, quality housing ladder.

- *Help elderly households meet their evolving housing needs and combat ageing unequally*: This includes, for instance, investments in tailored improvements to housing quality and accessibility (e.g. through tax relief, subsidies and/or grants) that can support individual preferences to age in place for as long as feasible; and considerations to facilitate co-operative living arrangements that bring together youth and seniors.

In addition to its far-reaching economic, social and health impacts, the COVID-19 pandemic has brought to the fore many of the housing challenges discussed in this report, providing a window into the disparities in access to good quality affordable housing. The pandemic renewed concerns over poor housing quality – particularly overcrowding -- in light of shelter-in-place and quarantine orders introduced in many countries. The widespread shift to teleworking and distance learning is not feasible for households who do not have a computer or access to the Internet at home.

At the same time, the economic fallout generated by COVID-19 crisis has also laid bare the scope and depth of housing instability and affordability gaps in many OECD countries. Without assistance, workers experiencing sudden income losses may struggle to pay their monthly rent, mortgage or utilities payments, while the homeless are unable to effectively shelter in place. Many government response packages to the crisis have aimed to help people remain in their homes or secure safe, temporary shelter during the course of the pandemic (OECD, 2020[11]). Such immediate (and in most cases, temporary) support has been essential to help vulnerable households cope during the crisis and maintain access to decent shelter. Yet as discussed in this report, moving forward, governments will need to develop longer-term, structural responses to overcome the persistent housing challenges and vulnerabilities.

References

Balestra, C. and R. Tonkin (2018), "Inequalities in household wealth across OECD countries: Evidence from the OECD Wealth Distribution Database", *OECD Statistics Working Papers*, No. 2018/01, OECD Publishing, Paris, https://dx.doi.org/10.1787/7e1bf673-en. [3]

Bonnet, C., B. Garbinti and S. Grobon (2019), *Rising inequalities in access to home ownership among young households in France, 1973-2013*, https://publications.banque-france.fr/sites/default/files/medias/documents/wp711.pdf (accessed on 5 July 2019). [21]

Causa, O. and J. Pichelmann (Forthcoming 2020), "Should I Stay or Should I Go? Housing and Residential Mobility across OECD Countries", *OECD Economics Department Working Papers*, http://dx.doi.org/ECO/CPE/WP1(2020)00. [10]

Causa, O. and N. Woloszko (2019), "Housing, wealth accumulation and wealth distribution: evidence and stylized facts", Economics Department - Economic Policy Committee, Working Party No. 1 on Macroeconomic and Structural Policy Analysis, http://dx.doi.org/ECO/CPE/WP1(2019)1. [4]

Chetty, R. et al. (2015), *The Impacts of Neighborhoods on Intergenerational Mobility: Childhood Exposure Effects and County-Level Estimates**, https://scholar.harvard.edu/files/hendren/files/nbhds_paper.pdf (accessed on 17 June 2019). [23]

Chetty, R. and N. Hendren (2018), "The Impacts of Neighborhoods on Intergenerational Mobility I: Childhood Exposure Effects*", *The Quarterly Journal of Economics*, Vol. 133/3, pp. 1107-1162, http://dx.doi.org/10.1093/qje/qjy007. [16]

Clarke, R., R. Fernandez and S. Königs (forthcoming), "Inequalities in household wealth: Drivers and policy implications", *OECD Social, Employment and Migration Working Papers*, OECD Publishing, Paris. [20]

Cribb, J., A. Hood and J. Hoyle (2018), *The decline of homeownership among young adults*, The Institute for Fiscal Studies, https://www.ifs.org.uk/uploads/publications/bns/BN224.pdf (accessed on 5 July 2019). [19]

Eurostat (2018), *Statistics Explained: Overcrowding rate*, https://ec.europa.eu/eurostat/statistics-explained/index.php/Glossary:Overcrowding_rate (accessed on 21 June 2019). [17]

Massey, D., J. Rothwell and T. Domina (2009), "The Changing Bases of Segregation in the United States", *Annals of the American Academy of Political and Social Science* 626, p. 1, http://dx.doi.org/10.1177/0002716209343558. [14]

OECD (2020), *Better data and policies to fight homelessness in the OECD. Policy Brief on Affordable Housing*, OECD Publishing, Paris, http://oe.cd/homelessness-2020. (accessed on 16 March 2020). [12]

OECD (2020), *Supporting people and companies to deal with the COVID-19 virus: Options for an immediate employment and social-policy response*, OECD Publishing, Paris, https://oecd.dam-broadcast.com/pm_7379_119_119686-962r78x4do.pdf (accessed on 25 March 2020). [11]

OECD (2019), *OECD Affordable Housing Database*, http://www.oecd.org/social/affordable-housing-database/. [22]

OECD (2019), *Society at a Glance 2019: OECD Social Indicators*, https://www.oecd-ilibrary.org/docserver/soc_glance-2019-en.pdf?expires=1560354363&id=id&accname=ocid84004878&checksum=899D5DEA8CA6220FEA9E89C2B381810E (accessed on 12 June 2019). [18]

OECD (2019), *Under Pressure: The Squeezed Middle Class*, OECD Publishing, Paris, https://dx.doi.org/10.1787/689afed1-en. [5]

OECD (2018), *Divided Cities: Understanding Intra-urban Inequalities*, OECD Publishing, Paris, https://dx.doi.org/10.1787/9789264300385-en. [15]

OECD (2018), *Opportunities for All: OECD Framework for Policy Action on Inclusive Growth*, https://www.oecd-ilibrary.org/docserver/9789264301665-en.pdf?expires=1559813226&id=id&accname=ocid84004878&checksum=FB84F54E2BA978AD3170920AA4FBD722 (accessed on 6 June 2019). [2]

OECD (2015), *All on Board: Making Inclusive Growth Happen*, OECD Publishing, Paris, https://dx.doi.org/10.1787/9789264218512-en. [1]

OECD (2011), *Economic Policy Reforms 2011: Going for Growth*, OECD Publishing, Paris, https://dx.doi.org/10.1787/growth-2011-en. [6]

Oswald, A. (2009), "The Housing Market and Europe's Unemployment: A Non-technical Paper*", in *Homeownership and the Labour Market in Europe*, Oxford University Press, http://dx.doi.org/10.1093/acprof:oso/9780199543946.003.0003. [9]

Sánchez, A. and D. Andrews (2011), "Residential Mobility and Public Policy in OECD Countries", *OECD Journal: Economic Studies*, Vol. 2011/11, http://dx.doi.org/10.1787/19952856. [7]

Sánchez, A. and D. Andrews (2011), "To Move or not to Move: What Drives Residential Mobility Rates in the OECD?", *OECD Economics Department Working Papers*, No. 846, http://dx.doi.org/ttps://doi.org/10.1787/18151973. [8]

van Ham, M. et al. (2016), "Spatial Segregation and Socio-Economic Mobility in European Cities", *IZA Discussion Paper* No. 10277, https://www.oecd.org/regional/makingcities-work-for-all-9789264263260-en.htm (accessed on 18 June 2019). [13]

Notes

1 Housing tenure is a key determinant of levels of wealth inequality within countries. Countries with higher levels of home ownership tend to exhibit lower wealth inequality, because housing wealth tends to be distributed much more equally than other assets (Balestra and Tonkin, 2018[3]; Causa and Woloszko, 2019[4]). Housing tends to equalise the distribution of wealth from a cross-country perspective, because housing represents a much higher source of wealth among middle-class households than at the top (Causa and Woloszko, 2019[4]).

2 The definition of overcrowding is based the EU-agreed definition (Eurostat, 2018[17]), which measures as the number of rooms per household member, taking into account different factors of household composition. For a full explanation, see: www.oecd.org/els/family/HC2-1-Living-space.pdf.

3 The authors define higher opportunity neighbourhoods as a commuting zone or county in which the children whose families are already living in the neighbourhood (e.g. sitting residents) have higher average incomes as adults (Chetty et al., 2015[23]).

2 Is the housing market an obstacle to inclusive growth? For whom?

This section outlines the extent to which the housing market can be a barrier to inclusive growth for some groups, such as low-income households, children, youth, seniors and the homeless. Low-income households are more likely to be overburdened by housing costs and record the highest rates of overcrowding. Children are among those most likely to live in poor quality housing and neighbourhoods, making it hard to ensure a good start in life. Today's youth most commonly live with their parents, facing increasingly limited opportunities in the housing market. An important share of seniors who do not own their homes outright pay over 40% of their income on housing. Meanwhile, the rate of homelessness has increased in a third of OECD countries, including among youth, families with children, and seniors in some countries.

Housing is a key dimension of inclusive growth, but some groups face bigger obstacles in the housing market than others.[1] This section explores the housing challenges of low-income households, children, youth, seniors, and the homeless, for whom reduced housing opportunities and poorer housing outcomes threaten to deepen inequalities across people, space and time.

2.1. Overall trends in the housing market

The housing sector in many OECD countries is changing on several fronts, with important implications for low-income and other vulnerable households. First, even though home ownership remains the dominant form of tenure for the majority of OECD households (Figure 2.1), this is changing in many countries. On average, in 2018 nearly 70% of households across the OECD either owned their dwelling outright or with a mortgage, while 28% rented a dwelling, either in the private rental market or as subsidised rental housing. As will be discussed below, the policy preference for home ownership in many OECD countries has contributed in part to the dominance of owner-occupied housing. However, the share of owner-occupied dwellings in the total housing stock has declined or stabilised in nearly all OECD countries since 2000 – thus before the global crisis, and especially for young people (Scanlon and Whitehead, 2004[1]; Arundel and Doling, 2017[2]; Whitehead and Williams, 2017[3]).

Second, the private rental sector is expanding and the age of renters is diversifying (Hulse, Parkinson and Martin, 2018[4]). In some countries, tenants are staying longer in private rental housing, underscoring its decline as a transitional tenure for young adults on their path towards home ownership, as well as a trend in older households remaining in or re-entering the rental market. In most OECD countries, private rental housing was the only tenure type that saw a consistent increase across all age groups since 2010 (with the exception of seniors over 65). The diversification of tenants in the private rental sector can in part be attributed to rising house prices that put home ownership out of reach for some households, as well as growing pressures on the social (subsidised) rental sector.

Third, as discussed in Section 1, housing is on average, across all income groups, the single-largest expenditure of households in the OECD (Figure 1.1, Panel A). The weight of housing in household budgets affects households' ability to spend or invest in other areas that matter for inclusive growth, such as education or health. Part of the reason lower-income households spend more on housing on average, relative to other income groups, is that housing is a necessary good and one of the first expenses that households need to cover. For some people, higher housing costs may not be an impediment to achieving greater satisfaction, but rather a means to achieving it: some households are willing to spend more to live in areas with better-performing schools or better air quality, which are key to improving outcomes for households and especially for children.

Fourth, estimates of consumption data suggest that people are spending more of their household budget on housing than they used to (Figure 1.1, Panel B).[2] On average across OECD countries for which estimates are available[3], the share of housing in household budgets – which covers housing costs (e.g. rent), regular maintenance and repairs, and utilities – rose by nearly 5 percentage points between 2005 and 2015. Over the past decade, the share of household budgets also increased for other key consumption items such as transport, health and education, yet to a lesser extent (a less than 1 percentage-point increase). Going back twenty years in time (1995-2015), albeit for a smaller subset of countries[4], the share of household spending on housing increased even further. Households were estimated to have spent almost 6 percentage points more of their budget on housing in 2015 relative to 1995, compared to just over 2 percentage points more on health, the budget item for which the next largest jump in spending was recorded.[5]

Figure 2.1. In most OECD countries, owning a home is much more common than renting

Share of households in different tenure types, in percent, 2018 or latest year available

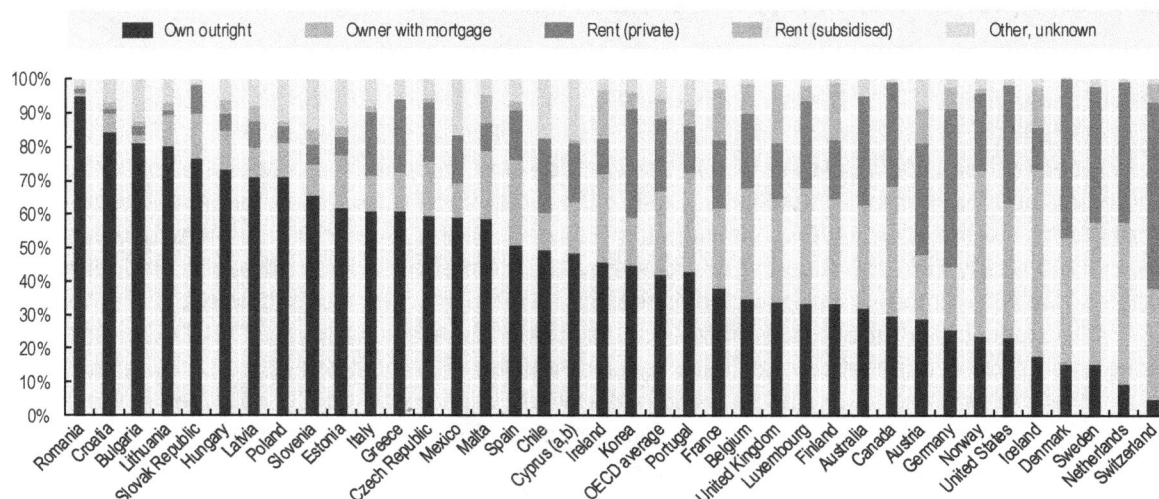

Note: Tenants renting at subsidised rent are lumped together with tenants renting at private rent in Australia, Canada, Chile, Denmark, Mexico, the Netherlands and the United States, and are not capturing the full extent of coverage in Sweden due to data limitations.
Source: OECD Affordable Housing Database (http://oe.cd/ahd), Indicator HM1.3. OECD calculations based on European Union Statistics on Income and Living Conditions (EU SILC) survey 2018 except for Ireland, the Slovak Republic, and the United Kingdom (2017), and Iceland (2016); the Household, Income and Labour Dynamics Survey (HILDA) for Australia (2017); the Canada Income Survey (CIS) for Canada (2016); Encuesta de Caracterización Socioeconómica Nacional (CASEN) for Chile (2017); the Korean Housing Survey (2017); Encuesta Nacional de Ingresos y Gastos de los Hogares (ENIGH) for Mexico (2016); American Community Survey (ACS) for the United States (2016).

Further, housing prices have increased over the past two decades, especially for renters. This can at least partly explain increased household spending on housing. On average, real house prices increased in 31 OECD countries between 2005 and 2019, with Colombia, Canada, Sweden and Israel recording the largest increases (over 80%) over this period (Figure 2.2 – Panel A). Seven OECD countries recorded a drop in real house prices over this period, most significantly in Greece, Italy and Spain. The evolution of rent prices across the OECD over this period features more uniform trends, with rent prices increasing in all but two OECD countries between 2005 and 2019 (Figure 2.2 – Panel B). Turkey, Lithuania, Iceland and Estonia recorded the largest increases (e.g. over 100%) over this period. Japan and Greece were the only two countries that saw a drop in real rent prices since 2005; however, in Greece, the drop in rent prices was nonetheless much smaller than that of real house prices (10% vs. 33% drop). High and rising rent prices also make it harder for tenants to save up for a down payment to purchase a home.

Figure 2.2. House prices increased in many OECD countries between 2005 and 2018

A. Real house price index, 2005 and 2018, 2015=100

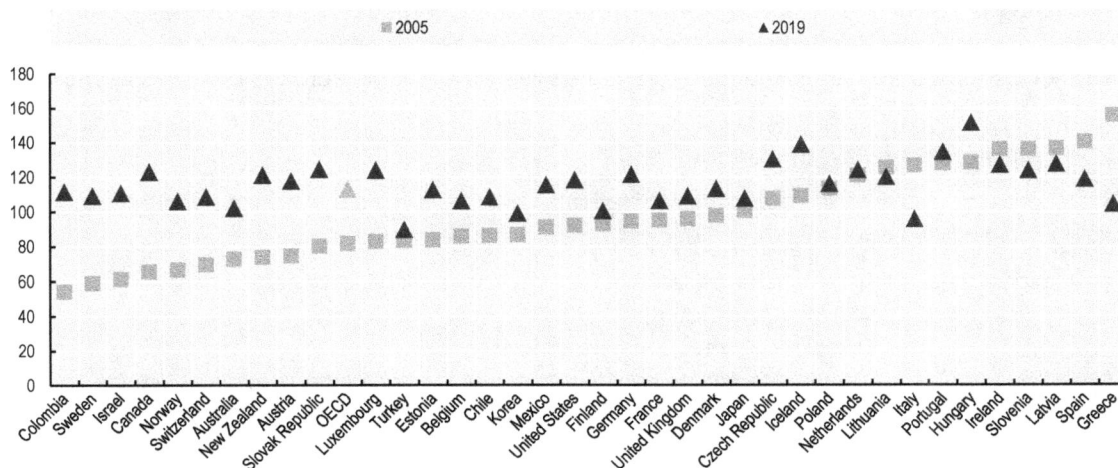

B. Rent price index, 2005 and 2018, 2015=100

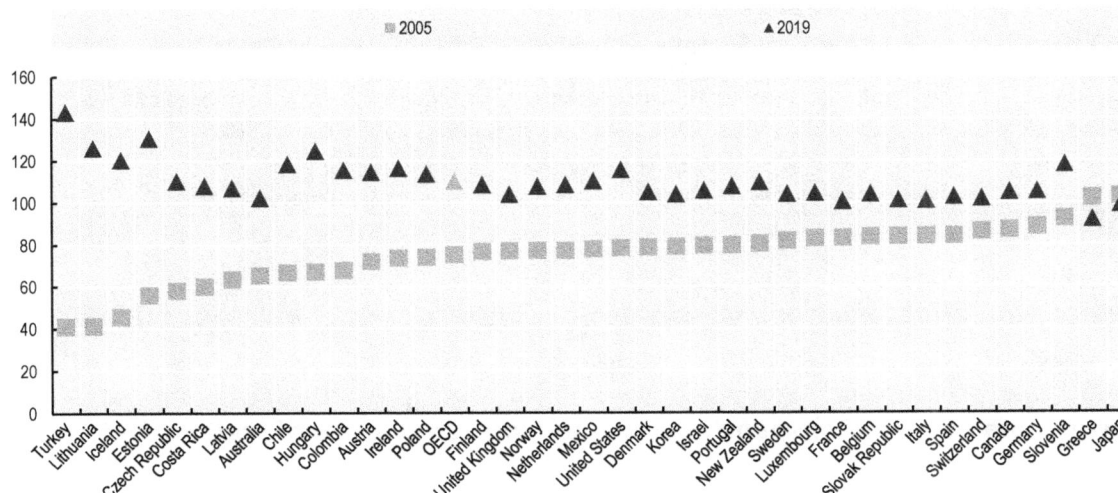

Note: House price indices, also called Residential Property Prices Indices (RPPIs), are index numbers measuring the rate at which the prices of all residential properties (flats, detached houses, terraced houses, etc.) purchased by households are changing over time. Both new and existing dwellings are covered if available, independently of their final use and their previous owners. Only market prices are considered. They include the price of the land on which residential buildings are located (see OECD et al. (2013[5])). For Panel A, 2005 data were not available in several countries; as such, data for the nearest available year were used: Latvia and Lithuania (2006), Luxembourg (2007), the Czech Republic (2008), Poland (2010) and Hungary (2007). For Panel B, 2005 data were not available in several countries; as such, data for the nearest available year were used: Norway (2008), Portugal (2010), Switzerland (2007), Germany (2007) and Greece (2010).
Source: OECD Affordable Housing Database (http://oe.cd/ahd), Indicator HM1.2. Calculations based on OECD Housing prices (indicator), https://dx.doi.org/10.1787/63008438-en (accessed on 20 September 2019).

Box 2.1 provides a summary of indicators of housing quality and affordability that are used in this report. These may provide a useful starting point for policy makers to assess the extent of housing market exclusion for different groups and regions in their country.

Box 2.1. Basic indicators of housing quality and affordability

Table 2.1 outlines a set of indicators of housing quality and affordability. Many of these data are available for a number of OECD countries in the OECD Affordable Housing Database (http://oe.cd/ahd), as well as other OECD databases. Other data are not as readily available across numerous countries.

Table 2.1. Indicators of housing quality and affordability

Category	Indicator
Housing context	Housing tenure rates (by income group, age, region)
Housing quality and conditions	Overcrowding (among families with children, by income group, by region)
	Housing deprivation rate
	Share of households living without basic facilities
Housing affordability	Share of household spending on housing costs (by income group, tenure, age cohort and region)
	Housing cost overburden rate (by income group, tenure, age cohort and region)
Housing wealth and liabilities	Share of households in negative equity (where liabilities exceed assets)
	Share of households in foreclosure *[NB: not discussed in this in report as limited cross-country comparative data]*
	Overcrowding (among families with children, by income group, by region)
	Housing deprivation rate
Housing stability	Homelessness rate (by age, by gender, by household type, by living arrangement [e.g. living rough, in shelter, with family/friends…], by jurisdiction)
	Number of evictions *[NB: not discussed in this in report as limited cross-country comparative data]*
Subjective indicators	Share of households satisfied with supply of affordable housing in their jurisdiction
	Share of households satisfied with their housing quality
	Share of individuals that consider quality housing as a major short-term concern

---

2.2. Good quality affordable housing is out of reach for many low-income households

2.2.1. Low-income households spend a large and increasing share of their budget on housing

On average across the OECD, low-income households spend the biggest share of their household budget on housing, much more so than middle- and upper-income households (Figure 1.1). As a result, they have fewer resources to invest in better housing or in other areas that could improve their life chances, such as education. Moreover, there is a large share of low-income households spending more than 40% on housing costs. The housing overburden rate, defined as the share of households spending more than 40% of their disposable income on housing costs[6], varies depending on whether households are renting a home or paying off a mortgage (Figure 2.3). In ten OECD countries, more than two out of five low-income renters in the private market spent over 40% of their disposable income on housing in 2018. The same share was reached for low-income owners with a mortgage in four OECD countries. In New Zealand and the United States, at least two out of five low-income people (regardless of tenure) spent over 40% of disposable income on rent or a mortgage in 2018. And while they tend to fare better than renters in the private market, at least three out of ten low-income renters in subsidised rental housing faced a housing cost overburden in Hungary, Finland and the United Kingdom (OECD, 2019[6]).

Figure 2.3. Low-income households face a significant housing cost burden

Share of population in the bottom quintile of the income distribution spending more than 40% of disposable income on mortgage and rent, by tenure, in percent, 2018 or latest year

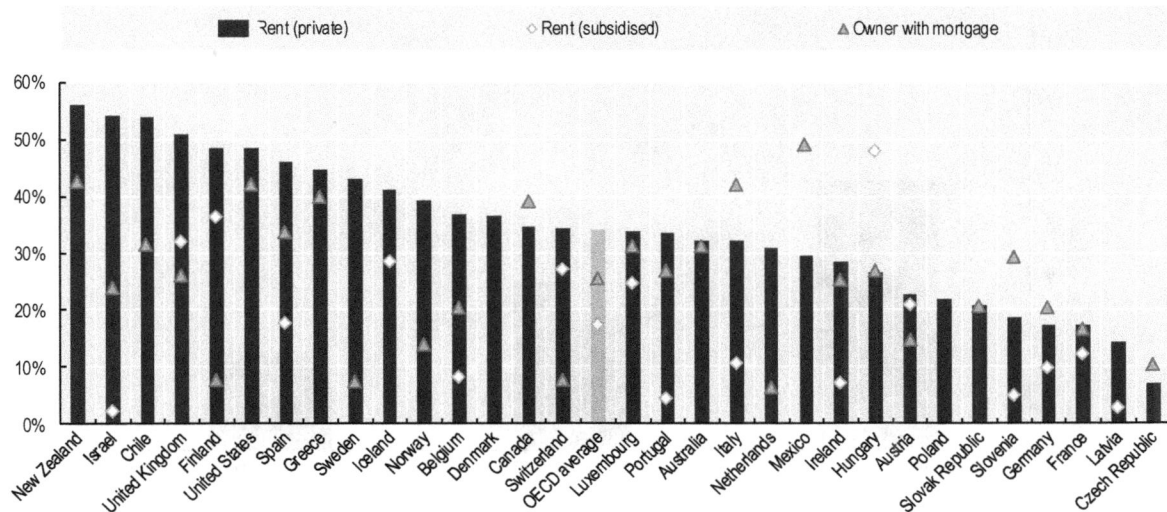

Note: 1. In Chile, Mexico, Korea and the United States gross income instead of disposable income is used due to data limitations. No data on mortgage principal repayments available for Denmark due to data limitations. 2. Results only shown if category composed of at least 100 observations.
Source: OECD Affordable Housing Database, Indicator HC1.2. OECD calculations based on European Union Statistics on Income and Living Conditions (EU SILC) survey 2018 except for Ireland, Malta, and the United Kingdom (2017), Iceland and Switzerland (2016) and the Slovak Republic (2015); the Household, Income and Labour Dynamics Survey (HILDA) for Australia (2017); the Canada Income Survey (CIS) for Canada (2016); Encuesta de Caracterización Socioeconómica Nacional (CASEN) for Chile (2017); calculations from the Bank of Israel for Israel (2017); the Korean Housing Survey (2012); Japan Household Panel Study (JHPS) for Japan (2016); Encuesta Nacional de Ingresos y Gastos de los Hogares (ENIGH) for Mexico (2014); Household Expenditure Survey (HES, Stats NZ) for New Zealand (2017); American Community Survey (ACS) for the United States (2016).

Moreover, while the share of spending on housing has increased for *all* households over the past decade, estimates of household consumption data suggest that low-income households have seen the most significant rise (Figure 2.4). On average across OECD countries for which estimates are available,[7] the share of housing costs in household budgets among the bottom quintile increased by more than 9 percentage points between 2005-2015, compared to an increase of around 5 percentage points for middle-income households and 3 percentage points for high-income households. Going back further in time for a smaller subset of countries[8], the weight of housing in household budgets increased by an estimated 13 percentage points for the bottom quintile between 1995 and 2015. This suggests that low-income households were seeing a larger share of their budgets go towards housing even well *before* the Global financial crisis (drawing on analysis prepared for OECD (2019[6])).

Figure 2.4. The share of housing spending has increased the most for low-income households

Percentage-point changes in share of household spending on housing by income group, OECD average, 1995-2015 and 2005-15

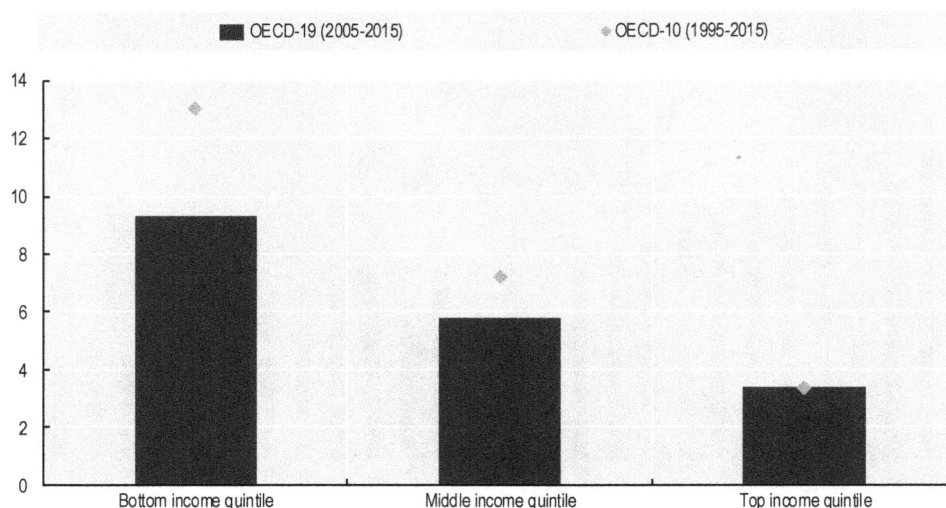

Note: OECD 19 unweighted average refers to the following countries: Austria, Belgium, Czech Republic, Germany, Finland, Greece, Hungary, Ireland, Lithuania, Luxembourg, Latvia, the Netherlands, Norway, Poland, Portugal, the Slovak Republic, Slovenia, Spain and Turkey. OECD 10 unweighted average refers to the following countries: Austria, Belgium, Finland, Germany, Greece, Ireland, Luxembourg, the Netherlands, Portugal and Spain. See explanatory note in Annex A for details on household the consumption expenditure data used in this report.
Source: (OECD, 2019[7]). Estimates based on microdata from the Eurostat Household Budget Surveys (EU HBS) 2010 and tabulations from the EU HBS 2015, 2005 and 1999 and 1994 for European countries except Spain (Encuesta de Presupuestos Familiares 2015).

2.2.2. Low-income households typically live in lower-quality dwellings

On average, low-income households have lower housing quality and are more likely to live in overcrowded conditions relative to those with higher incomes. Rates of overcrowding vary widely across countries, but in nearly all countries, households in the bottom quintile have a higher rate of overcrowding than those in the middle- or top-income quintile (Figure 2.5). In Mexico, Poland, Latvia and the Slovak Republic, more than 30% of low-income households are considered overcrowded. Overcrowding is also more likely to occur among renters, yet some countries also show high rates of overcrowding in owner-occupied homes (OECD, 2019[8]). The COVID-19 pandemic renewed concerns over overcrowding and other deficiencies in housing and neighbourhood quality, which can have adverse health effects (Box 2.2).

Figure 2.5. Overcrowding is more prevalent among low-income households relative to other income groups

Share of overcrowded households, by quintiles of the income distribution, in percent, 2018 or latest year available

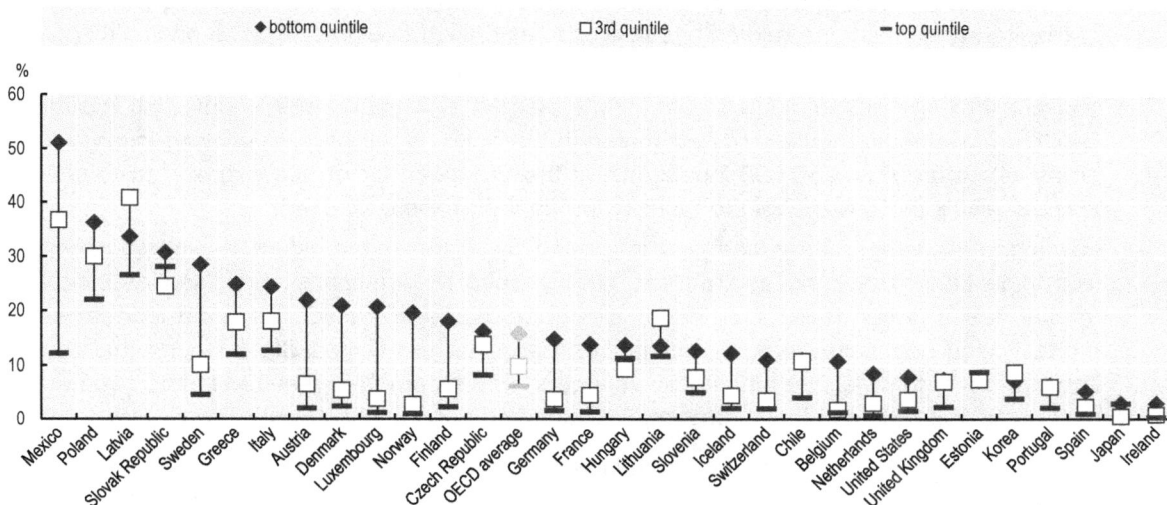

Note: 1. For Chile, Mexico, Denmark, the Netherlands and the United States no information on subsidized tenants due to data limitations. See section "Data and comparability issues" of Indicator HC2.1 on limits to comparability across countries due to the definition of rooms. 2. Low-income households are households in the bottom quintile of the (net) income distribution. In Chile, Mexico, Korea and the United States gross income is used due to data limitations. 3. Data for Japan only available on the respondent level due to data limitations. Results therefore refer to the population, rather than to households. 4. Data for Canada are adjusted by Statistics Canada based on the assumption of the presence of a kitchen in dwellings where it is expected. Income quintiles for Canada are based on adjusted after-tax household income.
Source: OECD Affordable Housing Database (http://oe.cd/ahd), Indicator HC2.1. OECD calculations based on European Union Statistics on Income and Living Conditions (EU SILC) survey 2018 except for Ireland and the Slovak Republic (2017), and Iceland and the United Kingdom (2016); calculations from Statistics Canada based on the 2016 Canada Census of Population for Canada; Encuesta de Caracterización Socioeconómica Nacional (CASEN) for Chile (2013); the German Socioeconomic Panel (GSOEP) for Germany (2014); the Korean Housing Survey (2017); the Japan Household Panel Study (JHPS) for Japan (2016); Encuesta Nacional de Ingresos y Gastos de los Hogares (ENIGH).

Box 2.2. Housing and health

People living in low quality housing and poorer neighbourhoods tend to have worse health outcomes, although it is difficult to establish direct causal relationships (Bonnefoy, 2007[9]; World Health Organization (WHO), 2018[10]; Fuller-Thomson, Hulchanski and Hwang, 2000[11]). Among the homeless, the health effects from a lack of shelter can be devastating. While "housing affects health and health affects housing," the former relationship has been studied to a much greater extent (Fuller-Thomson, Hulchanski and Hwang, 2000[11]). The quality and hygiene of the dwelling itself are important: poor air quality, high levels of noise, lack of ventilation and exposure to second-hand smoke, overcrowding, as well as the prevalence of mould, lead or asbestos can affect individuals' health (Mackenbach and Howden-Chapman, 2002[12]; World Health Organization (WHO), 2018[10]). As summarised in World Health Organization (2018[10]):

- Overcrowding can increase the risk of infectious diseases, namely tuberculosis. For instance, studies in Canada and New Zealand found that household overcrowding is associated with a higher incidence of tuberculosis (Wanyeki et al., 2006[13]; Baker et al., 2008[14]). More research is needed to assess the effects of overcrowding on health outcomes during the COVID-19 pandemic.

- Exposure to poor indoor air quality – which can result from the quality of a dwelling's ventilation system, its methods for cooking and heating, etc. – is associated with numerous negative health outcomes, including allergies, weakened immune system and cancer, as well as negative effects on reproductive, nervous and cardiovascular systems. One estimate suggests that dampness and mould in dwellings are associated with between a 30-50% increase in a range of respiratory and asthma-related health outcomes (Fisk, Lei-Gomez and Mendell, 2007[15]).

- Exposure to noise – and especially sustained exposure to noise – can lead to sleep disorders and auditory challenges, including hearing loss, and also challenges to physical and mental health and well-being. One study estimated that around 56 million people living in large urban areas with more than 250 000 inhabitants in the European Union are exposed to road traffic noise at levels that are thought to be risky to health (Babisch, 2012[16]).

- Low indoor air temperatures and poor insulation can increase the risk of respiratory conditions (e.g. high blood pressure, asthma and other respiratory infections and diseases) and poor mental health. Meanwhile, high indoor air temperatures are associated with higher risks of mortality and hospitalisations. For instance, a study in the United States found that thermal improvements to dwellings that stabilised indoor air temperatures resulted in improvements to occupants' reported health (Ahrentzen, Erickson and Fonseca, 2016[17]).

In many cases, children, the elderly and other vulnerable groups are at a greater risk of adverse health effects from low quality housing. This includes, for instance, the risk of lead poisoning from lead paint amongst children, as has been documented in the United States (Centers for Disease Control and Prevention (United States), 2018[18]). The adverse health risks from low quality housing will be exacerbated by population ageing and climate change with global temperatures continuing to rise and extreme weather events occurring with greater frequency and intensity. Spatial planning and urban design can both play a role in adapting housing and urban environments to help residents better withstand warming climates; moreover, local solutions can also be effective, such as the creation of public spaces that serve as "cooling centres" for the elderly and other vulnerable populations, as were introduced in Seoul, Korea (OECD, 2018[19]).

The broader neighbourhood environment – including proximity to pollution or crime, as well as access to quality schools and public services – also matters for individual health outcomes. Living in neighbourhoods that lack public spaces, green areas, parks, playgrounds or walking areas has been associated with insufficient physical exercise, increased prevalence of obesity, cognitive problems (among children), and decreased ability to socialise (Bonnefoy, 2007[9]). Outdoor air pollution caused more than 3 million premature deaths in 2010 (OECD, 2016[20]) – compared to roughly 1.3 million fatalities that year from road traffic accidents (World Health Organisation (WHO), 2018[21]) – with elderly people and children most vulnerable. Looking forward, outdoor air pollution could cause 6 to 9 million premature deaths a year by 2060 and cost 1% of global GDP (OECD, 2016[20]).

Housing status and conditions can also affect residents' mental health and well-being. Residential mobility can foster greater overall well-being and support broader inclusive growth objectives, in the case that individuals are able to move to higher-quality dwellings or neighbourhoods. However, there can be limits to the benefits of *frequent* residential mobility – particularly among children. High levels of residential mobility (e.g. frequency in changing residence) among young people have been associated with increased behavioural and emotional problems, increased teenage pregnancy rates, earlier illicit drug use and adolescent depression. Those effects may moreover cumulate and compound, reducing well-being at the neighbourhood, family and individual levels (Jelleyman and Spencer, 2008[22]). Studies in Canada and the United States have shown that children who move frequently may also experience less continuous healthcare provision and are more likely to use emergency health services. Moreover, significant levels of stress have also been documented in households facing housing instability, or financial instability as a result of high housing costs.

Meanwhile, the absence of a home has significant adverse health effects. Numerous studies have documented that homelessness drastically increases mortality rates. In France, researchers reported a 30 to 35-year difference in average age of death between the homeless and the general population (Cha, 2013[23]). A Polish study found that the average life span of a homeless person was 17.5 years shorter than that of the general population (Romaszko et al., 2017[24]). In Dublin, mortality rates were 3-10 times higher in homeless men and 6-10 times higher in homeless women compared with the general population (Ivers et al., 2019[25]). Further, homeless people are at increased risk of diseases, as well as mental illness, substance abuse, sexually transmitted diseases, and other health disorders (Fuller-Thomson, Hulchanski and Hwang, 2000[11]).

2.2.3. Housing is the biggest source of wealth and liabilities for low-income households

Housing has important implications for wealth. On the one hand, real estate assets overall tend to be more concentrated at the top of the income distribution, since higher-income households are more likely to own more expensive primary residences as well as invest in secondary residences. On the other hand, however, housing constitutes the largest source of wealth and the biggest financial liability among low-wealth households. Real-estate wealth makes up the biggest share of wealth among households in the bottom quintile, outweighing financial and other non-financial wealth in most OECD countries. The biggest shares of housing-related wealth among low-wealth households are found in the Netherlands, Denmark, Norway and Ireland (Figure 2.6). However, property liabilities (e.g. mortgages) among low-wealth households are larger, on average, than the level of housing assets, contributing to negative average net worth among low-wealth households in many OECD countries (Balestra and Tonkin, 2018[26]). Real estate tends to be the most important means to build wealth for low- and middle-wealth households; at the same time, however, this creates risks, as such households may be less able to draw on their wealth to absorb shocks in incomes, because real estate is not as easy to liquidate compared to other forms of wealth (Clarke, Fernandez and Königs, forthcoming[27]).

Mortgage debt can be both an opportunity and a risk for low-wealth households. On the one hand, it allows (particularly younger and lower-income) households to accumulate wealth, but, on the other hand, it also exposes them to financial risks. Lower-wealth households tend to be at a higher risk, whether measured in terms of solvency (their ability to pay back their mortgage) or liquidity (households' vulnerability to face difficulty in reimbursing mortgage debt in case of an economic shock). For instance, on average across the OECD, indebted households in the bottom quintile of the net wealth distribution record loan-to-value ratios (a solvency risk indicator) that exceed the conventional at-risk threshold value of 75% (Causa and Woloszko, 2019[28]). For all households, real-estate makes up the largest share of liabilities, on average, in most OECD countries (Figure 2.7).

Figure 2.6. Housing is the biggest source of wealth for low-wealth households – as well as their biggest financial liability

Composition of net wealth for poorest 20% of households, 2015 or latest available year. Wealth values (y-axis) are expressed in 2011 USD[1]

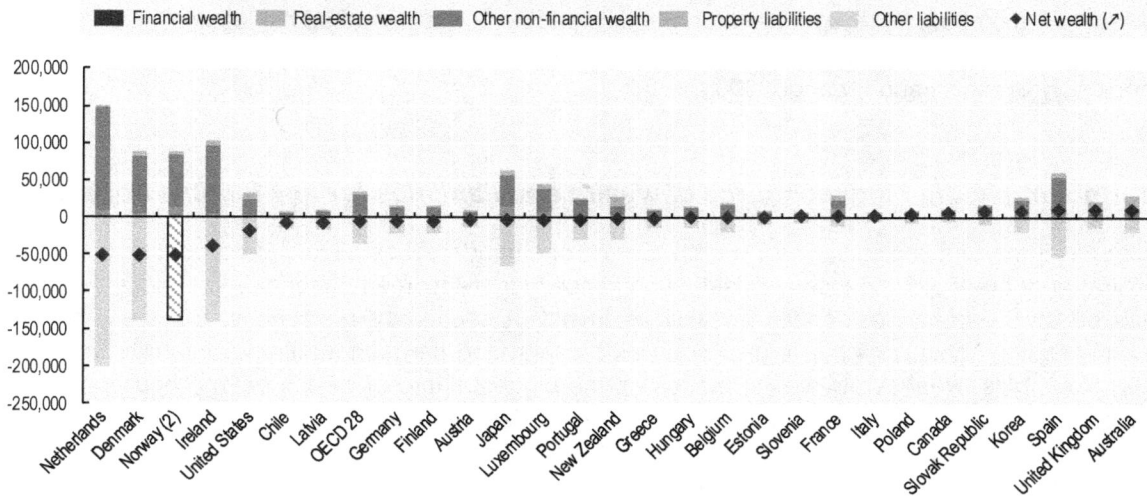

Note: 1. Wealth values are expressed in 2011 USD by, first, expressing values in prices of the same year (2011) through consumer price indices and, second, by converting national values into a common currency through the use of purchasing power parities for household consumption. 2. Data on the composition of household debt in Norway are not available, so total liabilities are shown.
Source: (Balestra and Tonkin, 2018[26]). Data from OECD Wealth Distribution Database.

Figure 2.7. Property liabilities make up the largest share of household debt in most OECD countries

Composition of household debt, 2015 or latest available year. Wealth values (y-axis) are expressed in 2011 USD

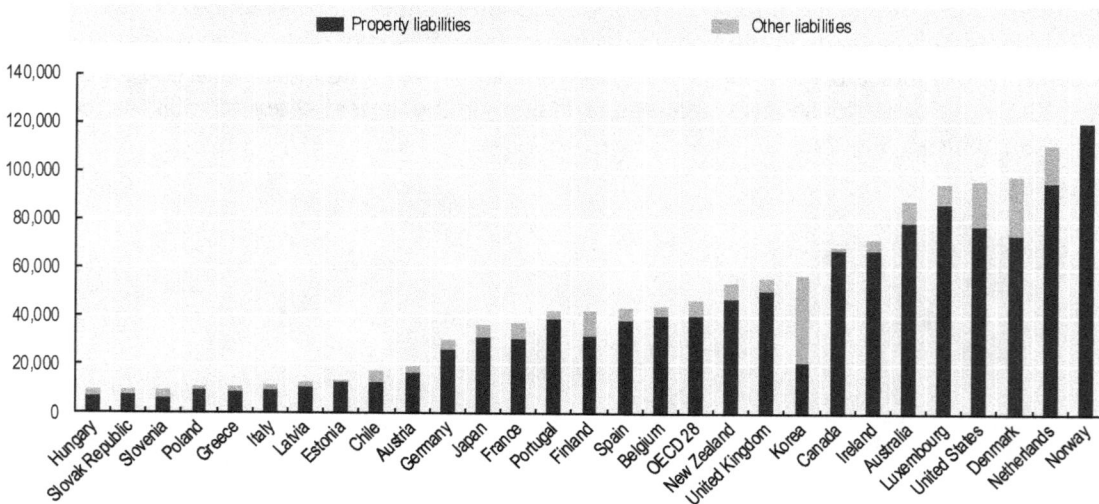

Note: Wealth values are expressed in 2011 USD by, first, expressing values in prices of the same year (2011) through consumer price indices and, second, by converting national values into a common currency through the use of purchasing power parities for household consumption. Data on the composition of household debt in Norway are not available, so total liabilities are shown.
Source: (Balestra and Tonkin, 2018[26]). Based on data from the OECD Wealth Distribution database (oe.cd/wealth).

High levels of real estate debt are not necessarily a problem, since they usually coincide with even higher housing wealth. However, over-indebtedness can pose risks to individuals and to the economy at large. High levels of debt relative to household income or to household assets can put households at risk of financial instability or default should asset (e.g. real estate) prices, interest rates or personal circumstances change. The Global Financial crisis contributed to over 9 million homeowners in the United States going through a foreclosure, surrendered their home to a lender or sold their home via a distress sale between 2006 and 2014 (Kusisto, 2015[29]). Too much debt can also create vulnerabilities for the economy as a whole, as was experienced during the global crisis (Balestra and Tonkin, 2018[26]), and weigh on long-term economic performance (Cournède, Denk and Hoeller, 2015[30]). Indeed, mortgage distress and defaults in the housing market were at the origins of the 2008 global financial crisis with lasting impacts on the housing market. Evidence from the United States suggests that the Global Financial crisis also resulted in unequal impacts across different types of households. Minority households, such as African-American and Hispanic households, suffered the most severe equity losses and experienced the sharpest increases in default as well as the biggest drops in home ownership rates in the aftermath of the Global Financial crisis (Gould Ellen and Dastrup, 2012[31]).

2.3. Many children face poor quality housing and housing instability

2.3.1. Housing and neighbourhood quality have long-lasting effects starting in childhood

Housing and neighbourhood quality matters, especially when children are young. Indeed, poor housing quality is a critical dimension of child poverty and represents one of the most common forms of material deprivation among children, compared to other dimensions, such as nutrition or clothing (Thévenon, 2018[32]). Research on intergenerational mobility from the United States finds that low-income children are most likely to succeed when they grow up in counties with less concentrated poverty, less income inequality, better schools, a larger share of two-parent families and lower crime rates (Chetty and Hendren, 2018[33]). Children who spend more of their early childhood years in higher-opportunity neighbourhoods[9] also earn more as adults.

For children, poor housing and neighbourhood quality can have an adverse impact on health and the home learning environment (Coley et al., 2013[34]; Evans, Saltzman and Cooperman, 2001[35]; Marcal and Fowler, 2015[36]). In OECD countries for which data are available, on average nearly 11% of children live in households with self-reported problems of crime, violence or vandalism in the local area; the share is higher among households with a low education level (15%) and among households in the lowest tertile of the income distribution (13%) (OECD, 2019[37]). Although it can be difficult to disentangle the neighbourhood from the socio-economic effect, the impact of one's childhood neighbourhood can be long lasting. Evidence from the United States and the United Kingdom finds that life expectancy can vary by decades across neighbourhoods, based on the neighbourhood's proximity to environmental and health hazards, the concentration of poverty and the level of racial segregation (OECD, 2016[38]).

The neighbourhood in which housing is situated shapes children's access to (quality) schools and educational opportunities. The quality of neighbourhood communities – in terms of peers, colleagues, and local authorities – and facilities can have a direct impact on early childhood outcomes (OECD, 2017[39]). The broader learning environment encompasses a child's home, neighbourhood and early childhood education and care services. Households tend to geographically cluster based on their incomes (see discussion of spatial segregation below) (OECD, 2018[40]), and the socio-economic segregation of neighbourhoods can reproduce itself in schools: OECD (2012[41]) reports that wealthier parents tend to avoid schools with a significant number of disadvantaged students. A study that followed individuals in England (United Kingdom) over time, at least part of the reason why poorer children fell behind their richer peers could be attributed to attending different secondary schools (Crawford, Macmillan and Vignoles, 2017[42]). Wealthier parents are more likely to exercise school choice and can enrol their children in good quality schools, compared to more disadvantaged parents who tend to exercise choice less and send their children to their local neighbourhood schools (OECD, 2012[41]). Research suggests the existence of peer effects, and that pupils from a low socio-economic background gain from attending a school with students from a more advantaged socio-economic background (Causa and Chapuis, 2009[43]).

The challenges associated with poor neighbourhood quality and limited access to opportunity are especially salient, given that income segregation and spatial inequality are high and on the rise in many OECD countries. Residential segregation occurs when individuals with shared characteristics, such as income level, race or ethnicity, are concentrated in a geographic space. While some level of residential segregation is natural, it becomes problematic when it results in the concentration of disadvantage in space – that is, in neighbourhoods with poor access to quality jobs and services – as this can affect individual outcomes much later in life, weighing on future generations and limiting social mobility (OECD, 2016[38]; OECD, 2018[44]). A comparison of segregation by income levels in twelve countries[10] yields considerable differences in spatial patterns within and across countries (OECD, 2018[44]). For instance, the most income-segregated cities in the Netherlands and France are at comparable levels with the least income-segregated cities in the United States (OECD, 2016[38]). OECD (2018[44]) found that income segregation tends to be higher in bigger, richer and more productive metropolitan areas. Segregation by income level has increased in recent decades in Europe and the United States (van Ham et al., 2016[45]; Massey, Rothwell and Domina, 2009[46]). These findings have particular importance for households with children, and suggest that interventions that focus on (young) children can have important generational effects.

2.3.2. Poor children are more likely to face poor housing quality

On average, more than 1 in 5 children between 0-17 years old live in an overcrowded household in European OECD countries, with considerable variation across countries (Figure 2.8). Over half of all children live in overcrowded households in Hungary, Latvia and Poland, compared to less than 8% in Ireland, the United Kingdom, the Netherlands, Norway and Finland. In all countries for which data are available, children in low-income households are much more likely than those in high-income households to face overcrowded conditions.

Even children who do not live in income-poor households can suffer from housing-related deprivation that relates either to the quality of the dwelling or the broader neighbourhood environment (such as noise or crime). For instance, one in five children in non-income poor households in France and Spain, and one in four non-income poor children in the United Kingdom, are faced with "multiple housing problems", a composite measure of housing quality that includes adequate lighting, quality of roof, presence of humidity or mould, ability to keep the dwelling adequately warm (Thévenon, 2018[32]).

Figure 2.8. Children in low-income households are more likely to be exposed to poor housing quality than children in higher-income households

Share of children (aged 0-17) living in overcrowded households in European OECD countries, by income group, percentages, 2017

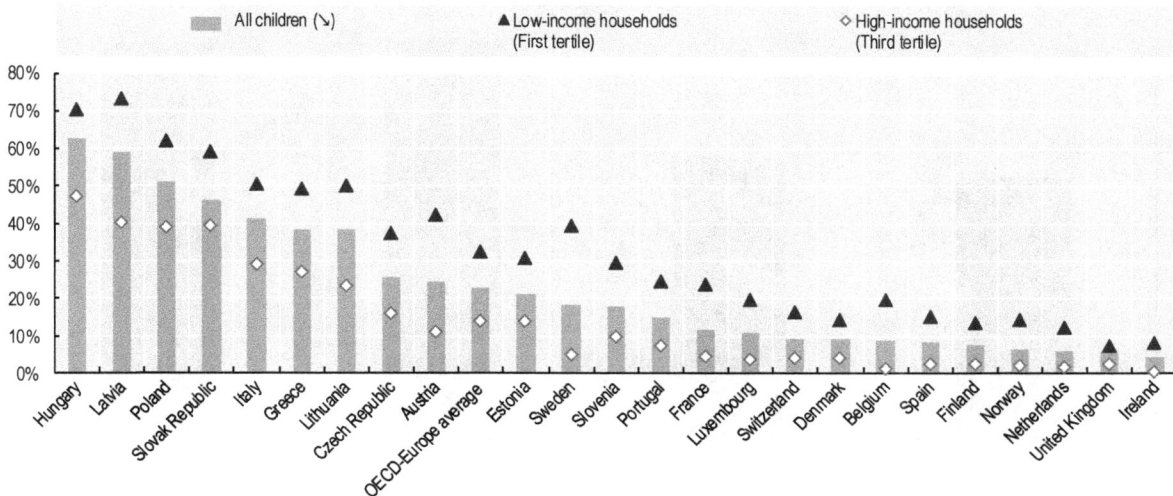

Note: 1. No information for Australia, Chile, Germany, Israel, Japan, Korea, Mexico, New Zealand, Turkey and United States due to data limitations. 2. Data for Switzerland refer to 2016.
Source: (OECD, 2019[47]). OECD Secretariat calculations based on the European Union Statistics on Income and Living Conditions (EU-SILC) survey, see OECD Child Well-Being Data Portal under www.oecd.org/els/family/child-well-being/data.

2.3.3. Many families with children are finding it hard to afford quality housing

The rising cost of housing means that young families with children – even those with median income levels – are finding it increasingly difficult to afford quality housing, including purchasing a home. Based on price data from capital cities across the OECD, OECD (2019[7]) finds that a median-income couple with two children must spend significantly more to purchase a modest-sized flat today than they would have 30 years ago, putting increasing pressures on household budgets and making home ownership less accessible to young families relative to previous generations (Figure 2.9). Real interest rates have fallen considerably since 1985, moderating somewhat the impact of house price increases on housing costs.

Figure 2.9. Today's families must pay considerably more to buy a flat than previous generations.

Number of years of annual income needed to buy a 60 square metre flat in the country's capital city or financial centre, for a median income couple with two children.

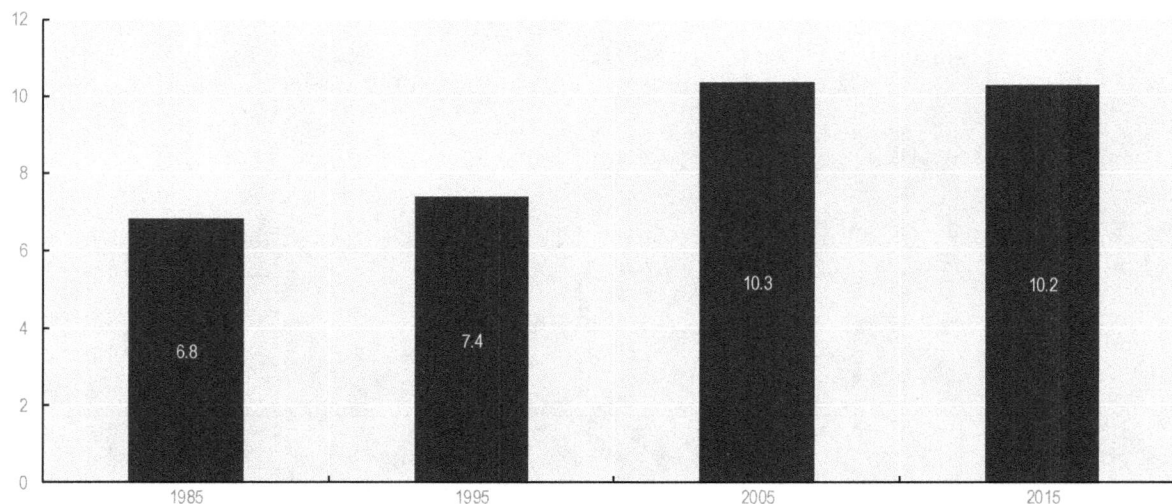

Note: Households composed of a couple and two children with median income. OECD average includes Australia, Canada, Denmark, Finland, France, Germany, Greece, Hungary, Israel, Italy, Netherlands, Norway, Sweden, Switzerland, the United Kingdom, and the United States. Source: (OECD, 2019[7]). Calculations based on data from EU-SILC (Europe), SLID and CIS (Canada), CPS March Supplement (United States) and LIS Data Center: Global Property Guide; OECD Residential Property Prices Indices (RPPIs).

2.4. Youth struggle to access quality, affordable housing of their own, risking a deepening of inter- and intra-generational inequality

Housing is one of several dimensions of well-being – along with employment opportunities – that have become more challenging for young adults in recent years, and threatens to deepen inter- and intra-generational inequalities. Frequently, today's youth have access to fewer quality, affordable housing opportunities than previous generations and they increasingly struggle to become homeowners, which limits their ability to build wealth. Low-income youth face even greater challenges than their higher-income peers in securing good quality housing, because they are not able to rely on family resources for support.

2.4.1. Facing reduced *opportunities* in the housing market, most young people still live with their parents

In a context of rising rents and house prices, several features of youth living arrangements are worth noting:

- Young adults aged 20-29 (e.g. those out of upper secondary schooling) are, on average across the OECD, most commonly living with their parents, though there is wide variation across countries (Figure 2.10). The biggest shares of youth living with their parents were recorded in Italy (75% in 2017), the Slovak Republic (74%) and Greece (74%), followed by Slovenia, Spain and Portugal (each around 70%). The Nordic countries are a notable exception, as only 10-20% of youth in Norway, Finland and Sweden live with their parents; they are more likely to be living with a partner or living alone.

- The trend in youth living with their parents appears to be on the rise in some OECD countries. For instance, between 2007 and 2014, there was a 12.5 percentage-point rise in the share of youth aged 15-29 living with their parents in France; the share also increased by nearly 9 percentage points in Hungary, nearly 6 percentage points in Italy, and almost 5 in Greece (OECD, 2016[48]; Lennartz, Arundel and Ronald, 2016[49]).

- Nearly 30% of youth (aged 20-29) live in a private rental dwelling; no other age group includes as large a share of renters. Just over two-thirds of youth (20-29) in the OECD live in owner-occupied homes (OECD, 2019[6]).

- Youth tend to move to urban areas, where housing costs have soared in recent decades. While urban areas in the OECD are attracting more new residents overall compared to rural areas, youth make up a large share of new urban dwellers. In Latvia, Estonia, Japan, Israel, Korea, Spain, Sweden, the Slovak Republic, Australia, the United Kingdom, the Czech Republic and Norway, more than 90% of young internal net migrants[11] moved to regions with a predominantly urban population in 2016 (OECD, 2018[50]).

In some countries, both low- and middle-income young households are finding home ownership increasingly out of reach. For instance, in the United Kingdom, home ownership rates among youth have dropped overall, and most significantly for those in the middle-income bracket: 65% of middle-income youth were homeowners in 1995-96, compared to just 27% two decades later (Cribb, Hood and Hoyle, 2018[51]). Clarke et al (forthcoming[27]) find that, relative to their peers in the past, younger people accumulate wealth less quickly, which may result from the rising age at labour market entry, less stable labour market prospects and slower earnings growth in the aftermath of the economic crisis.

Several factors have contributed to the decline in home ownership among young households, including high house prices, high transaction costs, insecure employment and low income levels (Whitehead and Williams, 2017[3]). On the one hand, rising house prices have made ownership increasingly unaffordable for young households, particularly relative to their income. For instance, in 2015-16, the average regional house price was four times the income of almost nine out of ten young adults in the United Kingdom; two decades earlier, this was true for less than half of young adults (Cribb, Hood and Hoyle, 2018[51]). On the other hand, notably in the aftermath of the Global Financial crisis, access to mortgages has become more difficult (particularly due to lower loan-to-value caps), while greater insecurity in economic and job conditions for youth are additional barriers to buying a home. Whitehead and Williams (2017[3]) suggest that the latter appears to have had a greater effect on home ownership rates among youth than the former. Arundel and Doling (2017[2]) argue that the decline in home ownership is not a temporary consequence of the global crisis, but given the increasing insecurity in the labour market (which especially affects youth) declining home ownership rates represent a more structural and sustained change in housing tenure arrangements.

Figure 2.10. In many OECD countries, youth most commonly live with their parents

Composition of household types amongst 20-29s in 2017, percentage

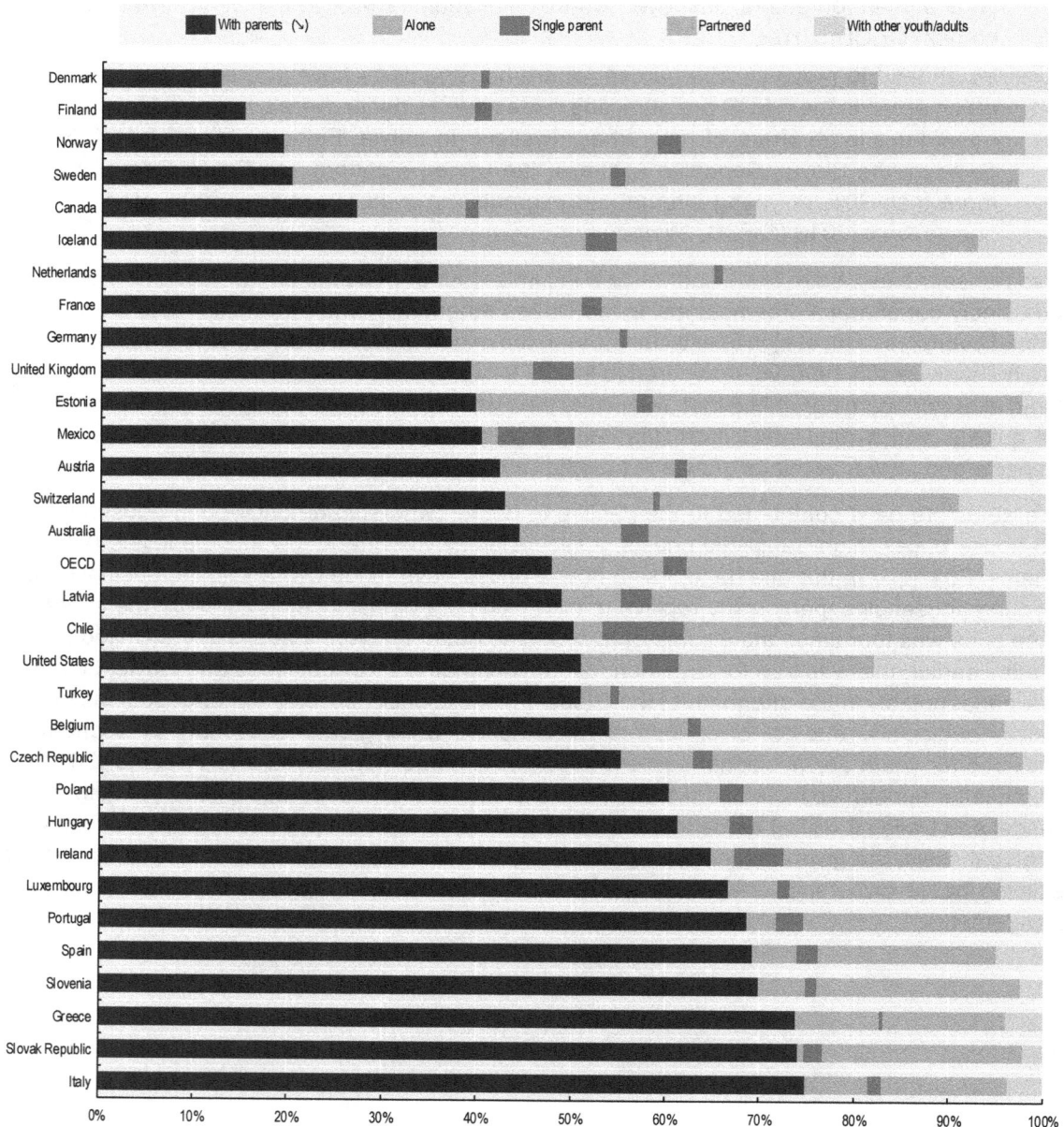

Note: Data refer to 2016 for Iceland, Ireland, Mexico, Switzerland, and United Kingdom 2015 for Turkey and 2011 for Canada. No information for Japan, Korea or New Zealand due to data limitations.
Source: OECD Affordable Housing Database (http://oe.cd/ahd), Indicator HM1.4. OECD calculations based on EU-SILC, HILDA (Australia), SLID (Canada), CASEN (Chile), ENIGH (Mexico) and CPS (United States).

2.4.2. Deepening intra-generational inequalities among youth who can rely on financial support from their families and those who cannot

In some OECD countries, young households increasingly rely on financial support from their families to purchase a home, which can in turn exacerbate intra-generational inequalities. In France, there is a growing gap in access to home ownership among affluent and low-income young households (aged 25 to

44): 32% of low-income young households were homeowners in 1973, compared to just 16% four decades later (Bonnet, Garbinti and Grobon, 2019[52]). This is in part driven by affluent young households increasingly benefitting from personal family financial support in the 2000s, which contributed to their capacity to purchase a home, while low-income households did not have similar levels of family support. Family support to buy a home also increased significantly in the United Kingdom: in 2014-15, three times as many buyers relied on support from inheritance relative to 1994-95 (Social Mobility Commission, 2016[53]). In Australia, around half of first-time buyers need financial support from their parents (Whitehead and Williams, 2017[3]).

2.4.3. Younger generations are more worried about their housing opportunities

It is not surprising, then, that access to quality affordable housing is a chief concern of young people. According to the 2018 OECD *Risks That Matter* survey, which asked over 22 000 people in 21 OECD countries about their social and economic risks[12], housing concerns were highest among younger people. On average, around a third of respondents aged 20 to 34 reported that securing or maintaining adequate housing was among their top three short-term concerns, with the share peaking at 40% among 25 to 29 year olds (Figure 2.11) (OECD, 2019[54]). In all countries but one (Norway), the share of youth identifying housing as a top short-term concern was higher than the share of the overall population. Israel, Lithuania, Estonia, Slovenia and Portugal recorded a more than 20-percentage point difference between youth and the overall population. These countries, in addition to Chile, Austria, Finland and Canada, registered the largest share of youth (e.g. over 40%) identifying housing as a top short-term concern.

Figure 2.11. Housing is a top concern for younger generations

Percent of respondents identifying "securing or maintaining adequate housing" as one of the top-three greatest short-term (over the next year or two) risks to themselves or their immediate family, by age group, unweighted cross-country average, 2018

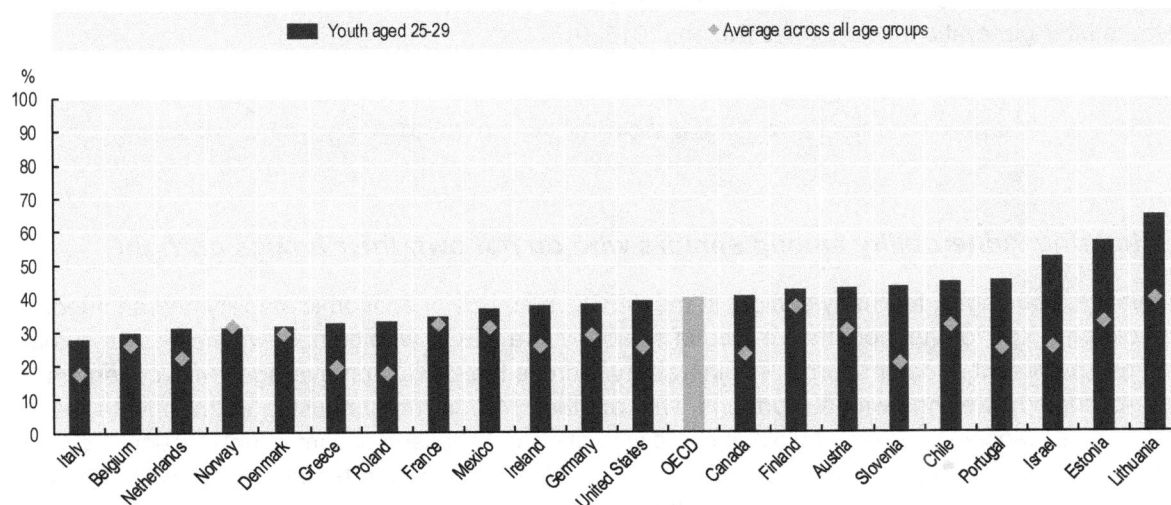

Note: Respondents were asked to identify the three greatest risks to themselves or their immediate family from a list of seven risks. Respondents had the option of selecting zero, one, two, or three risks.
Source: OECD Secretariat estimates based on the OECD *Risks That Matter* survey (OECD, 2019[54]).

2.4.4. Looking ahead: Youth in the face of increasing economic and housing instability relative to their peers of the past

Higher levels of vulnerability and instability among youth in the labour market have important implications for housing. When labour market instability is accompanied by lower wages or greater wage volatility, people face challenges to secure affordable housing in the rental housing market, where prices have continued to rise. Youth (aged 15-29), who were hit disproportionately hard by the Global Financial crisis, are more likely to work in temporary and atypical contracts that are easier to terminate (OECD, 2016[48]). Aurand et al. (2019[55]) reported that a minimum-wage worker would have to have three full-time minimum-wage jobs to afford paying rent for a two-bedroom apartment anywhere in the United States in 2019. Longer term employment instability can in turn weigh on opportunities for home ownership. Arundel and Doling (2017[2]) suggest that the decline in well-paid jobs with secure contracts – particularly among young adults – is reducing youth's access to home ownership. One reason is that secure job contracts are most appropriate for taking out housing loans. A study of six European countries finds that higher levels of employment insecurity reduce the chances of holding a mortgage in all countries (Dotti Sani Collegio Carlo Alberto et al., 2018[56]). Prospective homeowners are not the only ones made more vulnerable by increasingly flexible employment contracts, as landlords often require employment stability from prospective tenants.

Looking ahead, increased instability in housing, employment and other aspects of life for youth not only risks changing the structure of home ownership patterns in the future, but also exacerbating inter-generational inequality. On the one hand, Arundel and Doling (2017[2]) report that the cumulated trends of "delayed labour market entry, increased educational indebtedness, and a lack of well-paid and stable job opportunities" have created obstacles for youth to make traditional transitions into adulthood, including for housing. As a result, youth are struggling to get on a stable, quality housing ladder – including, but not limited to, home ownership. This can result in delayed household and family formation, and can also affect their access to quality schools (for their children), employment opportunities and wealth-building opportunities through home ownership. On the other hand, while rising house prices create challenges for young generations, older home-owning households tend to reap the benefits, which may ultimately exacerbate inter-generational disparities (Meen, 2018[57]).

2.5. The vulnerable elderly face exclusion as populations age and housing prices rise

2.5.1. Housing vulnerability among seniors who do not own their homes outright

At first glance, housing is, for many seniors in the OECD, a source of economic stability and an important asset in old age. Yet, for the more than a third of seniors in the OECD who do not own their home outright, housing can represent a major source of vulnerability. Across the OECD, on average, 14% of seniors live in owner-occupied dwellings with a mortgage, with another 14% in rental housing in the private market, 5% in subsidised (social) housing, and 5% in some type of institutionalised or communal housing. However, there is significant cross-country variation (Figure 2.12). More than one in ten seniors who do not live in homes that are owned outright[13] are overburdened by housing costs. In some countries, the share of seniors paying over 40% of their disposable income on housing can be much larger, reaching around 20% of all seniors in Australia, Belgium, Chile, Greece, Japan, Sweden and the United States, and 18% in the United Kingdom. There are important cross-country differences (see Table B.1 in Annex B). Seniors living in private rental housing are especially sensitive to increases in rental prices, as their income from pensions tends to increase more slowly than rent.

Because the majority of seniors own their home outright, they tend to be overrepresented among the "income-poor but asset-rich" households, and are more likely to be able to rely on their real estate assets in old age, even if their income does not continue to increase (Clarke, Fernandez and Königs, forthcoming[27]). This is a big difference compared to seniors who are *both* income- and asset-poor and are likely to suffer from old-age poverty because they cannot compensate their low incomes by drawing on wealth; this group may also find it harder to pay for caring expenditures (Clarke, Fernandez and Königs, forthcoming[27]). Heightened housing and economic vulnerability among seniors can have significant consequences, and in the most extreme cases, can lead to homelessness (see discussion below).

2.5.2. Large gaps in access to health and transport services among the elderly

There are large inequalities in access to health and transport services for elderly populations in the OECD, with considerable regional variation across countries (OECD, 2017[58]). For instance, OECD (2017[58]) found that the regional distribution of hospital beds and doctors does not match the localities where older people live in most OECD countries, and that physical proximity to the nearest hospital also varied widely across regions and is especially a challenge in more rural areas. In terms of access to public transport, which can facilitate the integration of older people into society as well as their ability to access health care and social and other services, there are important disparities in the share of the elderly population who can access public transport services within walking distance (OECD, 2017[58]).

2.5.3. Looking ahead: A housing stock that is ill adapted to an ageing population, and the implications of changing tenure patterns on wealth inequality

As populations across the OECD age (OECD, 2019[47]), the current housing stock appears ill adapted to the evolving needs of an ageing society. While housing quality and accessibility are important for all households, senior households have particular needs that may evolve over time. For elderly or disabled residents, the physical aspects of a dwelling can facilitate or hinder their daily activities. Well-adapted housing can enable ageing households to remain independently housed for longer, thereby reducing the need to transition to more costly supportive or institutionalised care (Slaug et al., 2017[59]). Adaptations to the dwelling can include eliminating stairs, widening doorways to allow for wheelchairs, ensuring that walls can withstand grab rails and providing an entrance-level toilet. Accessibility investments can have important health benefits, and do not necessarily imply significant net costs.[14]

Yet while data are far from comprehensive, much of the housing stock in the OECD is not equipped to allow seniors, to age in place (that is, to continue to live in their own homes) for as long as feasible, which is their preferred housing arrangement (OECD, 2017[58]). The Canada Mortgage Housing Corporation found that only one-quarter of all households and one-third of senior households had an accessible entrance (Canada Mortgage Housing Corporation, 2017[60]). Adapting dwellings or moving to a more suitable housing arrangement that meets the needs of seniors will be more difficult among ageing households who are poor.

Moving forward, housing for the elderly will be an increasingly pressing policy priority, given the current affordability pressures combined with ageing and inequality trends. Across the OECD, the risks of increasing inequality among the elderly have been building up, as demographic change and fiscal constraints are changing life prospects in old age (OECD, 2017[58]). In the OECD, on average one in seven people over the age of 76 is poor, and in many countries the over-76s are the age group most at risk of living in poverty (OECD, 2017[58]).

Figure 2.12. Seniors are most likely to live in dwellings they own outright

Share of the over-65 population by tenure status, 2017 or last year available

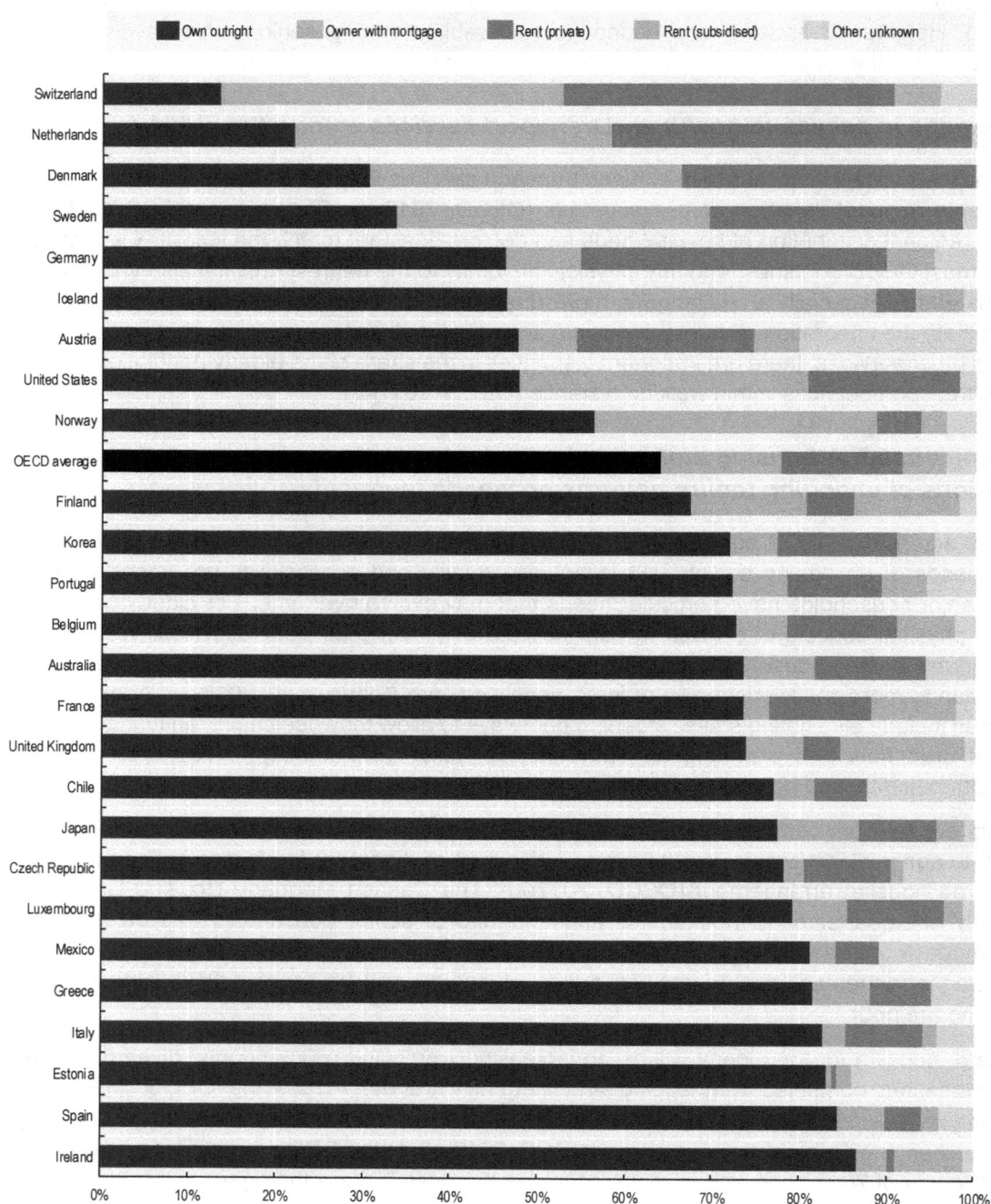

Note: OECD unweighted average.
Source: OECD calculations based on European Union Statistics on Income and Living Conditions (EU SILC) survey 2018 except for Ireland, the Slovak Republic, and the United Kingdom (2017), and Iceland (2016); the Household, Income and Labour Dynamics Survey (HILDA) for Australia (2017); Encuesta de Caracterización Socioeconómica Nacional (CASEN) for Chile (2017); the Korean Housing Survey (2017); Encuesta Nacional de Ingresos y Gastos de los Hogares (ENIGH) for Mexico (2016); American Community Survey (ACS) for the United States (2016).

2.6. The homeless population in some OECD countries is growing and increasingly diverse

2.6.1. The drivers of homelessness are multiple

The drivers of homelessness are multiple and complex, resulting from structural factors, institutional and systemic failures, individual circumstances – or a combination of these.

- *Structural factors* include tight housing market conditions, labour market changes, poverty, a shrinking social safety net, increased migration and, in particular, reductions in housing allowances. Research has identified a correlation between homelessness and rising housing costs; other studies have pointed to a link between homelessness levels and increasing rates of poverty and evictions.
- *Institutional and systemic failures* refer to the higher risk of homelessness and housing instability among people transitioning out of institutional settings, such as foster care, the criminal justice system, the military, or hospitals and mental health facilities. In France, for instance, around one in four homeless adults born in the country was previously in foster care or known to child welfare services.
- *Individual circumstances*, including traumatic events, such an eviction or job loss, a personal crisis (family break-up or domestic violence), child poverty, and health issues (mental health or addiction challenges) are also correlated with homelessness.

2.6.2. Homelessness is on the rise in a third of OECD countries

Homelessness is the most extreme form of housing and social exclusion. Homelessness has emerged as a pressing challenge across the OECD, in view of the increasing number of homeless people in many – but not all – OECD countries. According to the latest national statistics, there are roughly 1.9 million homeless people across 35 countries for which data are available, representing less than 1% of the total population in each country.[15] Due to methodological challenges and definitional differences across countries[16], this figure is likely an underestimate. In recent years, homelessness has risen in around one-third of OECD countries, and fallen or remained stable in a quarter of OECD countries. In many OECD countries, homelessness is concentrated in big cities. For instance, Dublin accounted for around 66% of the national homeless population in Ireland in 2019, even though it only represents about a quarter of the country's total population.

National trends in homelessness can also mask different developments across regions and cities within a country. For instance, a number of large metro areas have seen their homeless populations swell, even as national averages record more modest changes. In England (United Kingdom), despite a levelling off of rough sleepers nationally, their number has been increasing in London, Birmingham and Manchester. In Canada, homelessness rose in Toronto by 24% between 2008 and 2014, whilst decreasing in Calgary and Metro Vancouver by 62% and 39%, respectively. In the United States, homelessness increased by 57% in Los Angeles County and by 31% in New York City between 2012 and 2017, even as national trends were much more subdued (OECD, 2020[61]; 2019[6]).

2.6.3. The faces of the homeless are increasingly diverse

Policy makers must also keep in mind that people experience homelessness in different ways. A smaller, but more visible, share of the homeless population experiences prolonged periods of homelessness, or may transition in and out of homelessness over the course of several weeks, months or years (typically known as the "chronically homeless"). A larger share of the homeless population in most countries is "transitionally" or "temporarily" homeless, in that they are homeless for only a short period before finding a more stable housing solution.

In addition, the faces of the homeless are becoming increasingly diverse. Traditionally, single men have been more likely to be homeless. Although data on homelessness are hard to come by and difficult to compare across countries, homelessness among youth, families with children, and seniors has increased in some countries for which data are available. Further, in Australia, Canada, New Zealand and the United States, Indigenous populations are overrepresented among the homeless. Migrants make up a significant share of the homeless, but data are scarce.

Homelessness among families with children has risen – in some cases, significantly – in several OECD countries that monitor family homelessness. Homelessness among families with children almost quadrupled in Ireland between 2014 and 2018, from 407 to over 1 600 households (OECD, 2019[6]). Family homelessness in New Zealand increased by 44% between 2006 and 2013, representing nearly 21 800 individuals in 2013 (OECD, 2019[6]). Family homelessness in England (United Kingdom) increased by 42% between 2010 and 2017, representing over 44 000 households in 2017 (OECD, 2019[6]). In the United States, families with children represented one-third of the homeless population in 2018 (over 180 000 people in more than 56 300 families). Moreover, some U.S. states saw a significant rise in family homelessness: between 2007 and 2018, Massachusetts and Washington, D.C., experienced an increase in homelessness among families with children of more than 90%, while New York saw a rise of 51% over that period (US Department of Housing and Urban Development (HUD), 2018[62]). By contrast, family homelessness declined in Denmark and Finland in recent years (OECD, 2019[6]).

Children in homeless families are much more likely to suffer from negative impacts to their physical and mental health, and have a higher likelihood of poor educational outcomes (OECD, 2019[63]). Further, housing insecurity (which can take the form of housing unaffordability, frequent moves and homelessness) can contribute to child maltreatment, independent from poverty and economic hardships (Warren, 2015[64]). Lack of access to affordable and adequate housing compromises parents' ability to meet children's basic needs through material deprivation (OECD, 2019[63]).

Youth homelessness (among youth aged 15-29, unless otherwise indicated) is a growing concern in a number of OECD countries. However, in New Zealand, homeless youth represented around 1.1% of the total youth population in 2013 (11 076 homeless youth). In Australia, the share of homeless youth represented 0.77% of all youth in 2016 (38 277 homeless youth); 0.49% of the total youth population in Canada in 2016 (34 209 homeless youth); roughly 0.21% of all youth in Denmark in 2019 (1 928 homeless youth aged 18-29); and less than 0.15% of all youth in Finland and Ireland in 2018.

Further, among countries for which government data are available over time, youth homelessness has increased in Australia, Ireland and New Zealand, among others (OECD, 2019[6]). Ireland reported the largest increase, with a jump of 82% over just a four-year period, from 2014 to 2018. Denmark experienced an increase in youth homelessness (aged 18-29) of 43% between 2011 and 2017, but it has since declined between 2017 and 2019 (VIVE - Knowledge of Welfare The National Center for Welfare Research and Analysis, 2019[65]). Youth homelessness grew by 20% between 2011 and 2016 in Australia and by 23% between 2006 and 2013 in New Zealand (OECD, 2019[6]). In each of these countries except Ireland, youth homelessness grew faster than the growth in the overall homeless population. In some countries, youth ageing out of the state care system (such as foster care), for lack of transitional solutions upon becoming adults, end up homeless: in France, for instance, around one in four homeless adults born in the country was previously in foster care or known to child welfare services (Fondation Abbé Pierre, 2019[66]). Meanwhile, homelessness dropped among youth in Canada (by 17% between 2011 and 2016), Finland (by 25% between 2019 and 2018), and England (United Kingdom) (by 20% among 16-24 year olds between 2010 and 2017) (OECD, 2019[6]).

While cross-national data are scarce, homelessness among seniors has risen in several OECD countries. In Canada, while seniors make up only a small share of users of homeless shelters, the number of seniors using emergency shelters increased by about 50% from 2005 to 2016 (Government of Canada, 2019[67]). England (United Kingdom) recorded a ten-year high of homeless people over the age of 60 in 2018, with the share of homeless seniors more than doubling in eight years (Bulman, 2018[68]). In New York City, homelessness among seniors has more than tripled over the past decade, with the waiting list for affordable senior housing reaching up to seven years in some cases (CBS New York, 2019[69]).

References

Ahrentzen, S., J. Erickson and E. Fonseca (2016), "Thermal and health outcomes of energy efficiency retrofits of homes of older adults", *Indoor Air*, Vol. 26/4, pp. 582-593, http://dx.doi.org/10.1111/ina.12239. [17]

Arundel, R. and J. Doling (2017), "The end of mass homeownership? Changes in labour markets and housing tenure opportunities across Europe", *Journal of Housing and the Built Environment*, Vol. 32/4, pp. 649-672, http://dx.doi.org/10.1007/s10901-017-9551-8. [2]

Aurand, A. et al. (2019), *Out of Reach 2019*, National Low Income Housing Coalition, http://www.nlihc.org/oor (accessed on 20 June 2019). [55]

Babisch, W. (2012), *Exposure to environmental noise: risks for health and the environment. Workshop on "Sound level of motor vehicles"*, http://www.europarl.europa.eu/document/activities/cont/201205/20120524ATT45762/201205 24ATT45762EN.pdf (accessed on 19 September 2019). [16]

Baker, M. et al. (2008), "Tuberculosis associated with household crowding in a developed country", *Journal of Epidemiology Community Health*, Vol. 62/8, pp. 715-721, https://jech.bmj.com/content/jech/62/8/715.full.pdf (accessed on 19 September 2019). [14]

Balestra, C. and R. Tonkin (2018), "Inequalities in household wealth across OECD countries: Evidence from the OECD Wealth Distribution Database", *OECD Statistics Working Papers*, No. 2018/01, OECD Publishing, Paris, https://dx.doi.org/10.1787/7e1bf673-en. [26]

Bonnefoy, X. (2007), *Nos. 3/4, 2007 'Inadequate housing and health: an overview*, http://citeseerx.ist.psu.edu/viewdoc/download?doi=10.1.1.462.6443&rep=rep1&type=pdf (accessed on 17 June 2019). [9]

Bonnet, C., B. Garbinti and S. Grobon (2019), *Rising inequalities in access to home ownership among young households in France, 1973-2013*, https://publications.banque-france.fr/sites/default/files/medias/documents/wp711.pdf (accessed on 5 July 2019). [52]

Bulman, M. (2018), *Number of homeless pensioners in England hits 10-year high, figures show*, The Independent, https://www.independent.co.uk/news/uk/home-news/homeless-pensioners-elderly-single-parent-household-housing-shelter-figures-a8419241.html (accessed on 4 July 2019). [68]

Canada Mortgage Housing Corporation (2017), *Research Insight: Accessibility of Canadian Seniors' Homes*, http://peterkubiczekteam.com/wp-content/uploads/69126.pdf (accessed on 4 July 2019). [60]

Causa, O. and C. Chapuis (2009), "Equity in Student Achievement Across OECD Countries: An Investigation of the Role of Policies", *OECD Economics Department Working Papers*, No. 708, OECD Publishing, Paris, https://dx.doi.org/10.1787/223056645650. [43]

Causa, O. and N. Woloszko (2019), "Housing, wealth accumulation and wealth distribution: evidence and stylized facts", Economics Department - Economic Policy Committee, Working Party No. 1 on Macroeconomic and Structural Policy Analysis, http://dx.doi.org/ECO/CPE/WP1(2019)1. [28]

CBS New York (2019), *Finding Affordable Housing In NYC Is Hard, It's Almost Impossible If You're A Senior – CBS New York*, CBS New York, https://newyork.cbslocal.com/2019/06/12/affordable-housing-nyc-seniors/ (accessed on 4 July 2019). [69]

Centers for Disease Control and Prevention (United States) (2018), *Childhood Lead Poisoning*, https://ephtracking.cdc.gov/showCommunityDesignAddLinkChildhoodLeadPoisoning.action (accessed on 12 March 2020). [18]

Cha, O. (2013), *La santé des sans-abri - Health of the homeless*, Bulletin de l'Académie Nationale de Médecine. [23]

Chetty, R. et al. (2015), *The Impacts of Neighborhoods on Intergenerational Mobility: Childhood Exposure Effects and County-Level Estimates*, https://scholar.harvard.edu/files/hendren/files/nbhds_paper.pdf (accessed on 17 June 2019). [71]

Chetty, R. and N. Hendren (2018), "The Impacts of Neighborhoods on Intergenerational Mobility I: Childhood Exposure Effects*", *The Quarterly Journal of Economics*, Vol. 133/3, pp. 1107-1162, http://dx.doi.org/10.1093/qje/qjy007. [33]

Clarke, R., R. Fernandez and S. Königs (forthcoming), *Inequalities in household wealth: Drivers and policy implications*, OECD Publising, Paris. [27]

Coley, R. et al. (2013), "Relations between housing characteristics and the well-being of low-income children and adolescents.", *Developmental Psychology*, Vol. 49/9, pp. 1775-1789, http://dx.doi.org/10.1037/a0031033. [34]

Cournède, B., O. Denk and P. Hoeller (2015), "Finance and Inclusive Growth", *OECD Economic Policy Papers*, No. 14, OECD Publishing, Paris, https://dx.doi.org/10.1787/5js06pbhf28s-en. [30]

Crawford, C., L. Macmillan and A. Vignoles (2017), "When and why do initially high-achieving poor children fall behind?", *Oxford Review of Education*, Vol. 43/1, pp. 88-108, http://dx.doi.org/10.1080/03054985.2016.1240672. [42]

Cribb, J., A. Hood and J. Hoyle (2018), *The decline of homeownership among young adults*, The Institute for Fiscal Studies, https://www.ifs.org.uk/uploads/publications/bns/BN224.pdf (accessed on 5 July 2019). [51]

Dotti Sani Collegio Carlo Alberto, G. et al. (2018), "Two hearts and a loan? Mortgages, employment insecurity and earnings among young couples in six European countries", *Urban Studies Journal Limited*, Vol. 55/11, pp. 2451-2469, http://dx.doi.org/10.1177/0042098017717211. [56]

Eriksen, M., N. Greenhalgh-Stanley and G. Engelhardt (2015), "Home safety, accessibility, and elderly health: Evidence from falls", *Journal of Urban Economics*, Vol. 87, pp. 14-24, http://dx.doi.org/10.1016/J.JUE.2015.02.003. [70]

Evans, G., H. Saltzman and J. Cooperman (2001), "Housing Quality and Children's Socioemotional Health", *Environment and Behavior*, Vol. 33/3, pp. 389-399, http://dx.doi.org/10.1177/00139160121973043. [35]

Fisk, W., Q. Lei-Gomez and M. Mendell (2007), "Meta-analyses of the associations of respiratory health effects with dampness and mold in homes", *Indoor Air*, Vol. 17/4, pp. 284-296, http://dx.doi.org/10.1111/j.1600-0668.2007.00475.x. [15]

Fondation Abbé Pierre (2019), *L'état du mal-logement en France 2019 : Rapport annuel #24*, https://www.fondation-abbe-pierre.fr/documents/pdf/rapport_complet_etat_du_mal_logement_2019_def_web.pdf (accessed on 14 May 2019). [66]

Fuller-Thomson, E., J. Hulchanski and S. Hwang (2000), "The housing/health relationship: What do we know?", *Reviews on environmental health*, Vol. 15/1-2, pp. 109-33, http://www.ncbi.nlm.nih.gov/pubmed/10939088 (accessed on 17 June 2019). [11]

Gould Ellen, I. and S. Dastrup (2012), *Housing and the Great Recession*, The Russel Sage Foundation and the Stanford Center on Poverty and Inequality. [31]

Government of Canada (2019), *Highlights of the National Shelter Study 2005 to 2016 - Canada.ca*, https://www.canada.ca/en/employment-social-development/programs/homelessness/reports-shelter-2016.html#h4 (accessed on 17 December 2019). [67]

Hulse, K., S. Parkinson and C. Martin (2018), "Inquiry into the future of the private rental sector", *AHURI Final Report* 303, http://dx.doi.org/10.18408/ahuri-5112001. [4]

Ivers, J. et al. (2019), "Five-year standardised mortality ratios in a cohort of homeless people in Dublin.", *BMJ open*, Vol. 9/1, p. e023010, http://dx.doi.org/10.1136/bmjopen-2018-023010. [25]

Jelleyman, T. and N. Spencer (2008), "Residential mobility in childhood and health outcomes: a systematic review", *J Epidemiol Community Health*, Vol. 62, pp. 584-592, http://dx.doi.org/10.1136/jech.2007.060103. [22]

Kusisto, L. (2015), *Many Who Lost Homes to Foreclosure in Last Decade Won't Return — NAR*, https://www.wsj.com/articles/many-who-lost-homes-to-foreclosure-in-last-decade-wont-return-nar-1429548640. [29]

Lennartz, C., R. Arundel and R. Ronald (2016), "Younger Adults and Homeownership in Europe Through the Global Financial Crisis", *Population, Space and Place*, Vol. 22/8, pp. 823-835, http://dx.doi.org/10.1002/psp.1961. [49]

Mackenbach, J. and P. Howden-Chapman (2002), "Houses, neighbourhoods and health", *European Journal of Public Health*, Vol. 12, https://academic.oup.com/eurpub/article-abstract/12/3/161/497840 (accessed on 17 June 2019). [12]

Marcal, K. and P. Fowler (2015), *Housing and Child Well-Being*, Center for Social Development, George Warren Brown School of Social Work, https://openscholarship.wustl.edu/cgi/viewcontent.cgi?article=1805&context=csd_research (accessed on 15 July 2019). [36]

Massey, D., J. Rothwell and T. Domina (2009), "The Changing Bases of Segregation in the United States", *Annals of the American Academy of Political and Social Science* 626, p. 1, http://dx.doi.org/10.1177/0002716209343558. [46]

Meen, G. (2018), *How should housing affordability be measured?*, UK Collaborative Centre for Housing Evidence, http://housingevidence.ac.uk/wp-content/uploads/2018/09/R2018_02_01_How_to_measure_affordability.pdf (accessed on 22 July 2019). [57]

OECD (2020), *Better data and policies to fight homelessness in the OECD. Policy Brief on Affordable Housing*, OECD Publishing, Paris, http://oe.cd/homelessness-2020. (accessed on 16 March 2020). [61]

OECD (2019), *Affordable Housing Database - OECD*, http://www.oecd.org/social/affordable-housing-database.htm (accessed on 4 December 2018). [8]

OECD (2019), *Changing the Odds for Vulnerable Children: Building Opportunities and Resilience*, OECD Publishing, Paris, https://dx.doi.org/10.1787/a2e8796c-en. [63]

OECD (2019), *OECD Affordable Housing Database*, http://www.oecd.org/social/affordable-housing-database/. [6]

OECD (2019), *OECD Child Well-Being Data Portal*, http://www.oecd.org/els/family/child-well-being/data/ (accessed on 14 May 2019). [37]

OECD (2019), *Risks that Matter*, https://www.oecd.org/els/soc/Risks-That-Matter-2018-Main-Findings.pdf (accessed on 2 May 2019). [54]

OECD (2019), *Society at a Glance 2019: OECD Social Indicators*, https://doi.org/10.1787/soc_glance-2019-en (accessed on 12 June 2019). [47]

OECD (2019), *Under Pressure: The Squeezed Middle Class*, OECD Publishing, Paris, https://dx.doi.org/10.1787/689afed1-en. [7]

OECD (2018), *A Broken Social Elevator? How to Promote Social Mobility*, OECD Publishing, Paris, https://dx.doi.org/10.1787/9789264301085-en. [40]

OECD (2018), *Divided Cities: Understanding Intra-urban Inequalities*, OECD Publishing, Paris, https://dx.doi.org/10.1787/9789264300385-en. [44]

OECD (2018), *Inclusive Growth in Seoul, Korea*, OECD Publishing, Paris, https://dx.doi.org/10.1787/9789264290198-en. [19]

OECD (2018), *OECD Regions and Cities at a Glance 2018*, OECD Publishing, Paris, https://dx.doi.org/10.1787/reg_cit_glance-2018-en. [50]

OECD (2017), *Educational Opportunity for All: Overcoming Inequality throughout the Life Course*, Educational Research and Innovation, OECD Publishing, Paris, https://dx.doi.org/10.1787/9789264287457-en. [39]

OECD (2017), *Preventing Ageing Unequally*, OECD Publishing, Paris, https://dx.doi.org/10.1787/9789264279087-en. [58]

OECD (2016), *Making Cities Work for All: Data and Actions for Inclusive Growth*, OECD Publishing, Paris, https://dx.doi.org/10.1787/9789264263260-en. [38]

OECD (2016), *Society at a Glance 2016: OECD Social Indicators*, https://doi.org/10.1787/9789264261488-en (accessed on 20 June 2019). [48]

OECD (2016), *The Economic Consequences of Outdoor Air Pollution*, OECD Publishing, Paris, https://dx.doi.org/10.1787/9789264257474-en. [20]

OECD (2012), *Equity and Quality in Education: Supporting Disadvantaged Students and Schools*, OECD Publishing, Paris, https://dx.doi.org/10.1787/9789264130852-en. [41]

OECD et al. (2013), *Handbook on Residential Property Prices Indices (RPPIs)*, http://publications.europa.eu/others/agents/index_en.htm (accessed on 16 March 2020). [5]

Romaszko, J. et al. (2017), "Mortality among the homeless: Causes and meteorological relationships.", *PloS one*, Vol. 12/12, p. e0189938, http://dx.doi.org/10.1371/journal.pone.0189938. [24]

Scanlon, K. and C. Whitehead (2004), *International trends in housing tenure and mortgage finance*, Council of Mortgage Lenders, http://www.urbancenter.utoronto.ca/pdfs/elibrary/CML_Inter-Trends-Housing-Te.pdf (accessed on 8 July 2019). [1]

Slaug, B. et al. (2017), "Improved Housing Accessibility for Older People in Sweden and Germany: Short Term Costs and Long-Term Gains", *International Journal of Environmental Research and Public Health*, Vol. 14/964, http://dx.doi.org/10.3390/ijerph14090964. [59]

Social Mobility Commission (2016), *State of the Nation 2016: Social Mobility in Great Britain*, http://www.gov.uk/government/publications (accessed on 5 July 2019). [53]

Thévenon, O. (2018), "Child poverty in the OECD: Trends, determinants and policies to tackle it", *OECD Social, Employment and Migration Working Papers* 218, https://doi.org/10.1787/c69de229-en. [32]

US Department of Housing and Urban Development (HUD) (2018), *The 2018 Annual Homeless Assessment Report (AHAR) to Congress, Part 1: Point-in-Time Estimates of Homelessness*, https://files.hudexchange.info/resources/documents/2018-AHAR-Part-1.pdf (accessed on 21 June 2019). [62]

van Ham, M. et al. (2016), "Spatial Segregation and Socio-Economic Mobility in European Cities", *IZA Discussion Paper* No. 10277, https://www.oecd.org/regional/makingcities-work-for-all-9789264263260-en.htm (accessed on 18 June 2019). [45]

VIVE - Knowledge of Welfare The National Center for Welfare Research and Analysis (2019), *Homelessness in Denmark 2019: National mapping.* [65]

Wanyeki, I. et al. (2006), "Dwellings, crowding, and tuberculosis in Montreal", *Social Science & Medicine*, Vol. 63/2, pp. 501-511, http://dx.doi.org/10.1016/J.SOCSCIMED.2005.12.015. [13]

Warren, E. (2015), "Housing Insecurity, Maternal Stress, and Child Maltreatment: An Application [64] of the Family Stress Model", *Social Service Review*, Vol. 89/1, https://www.journals.uchicago.edu/doi/full/10.1086/680043.

Whitehead, C. and P. Williams (2017), "Changes in the regulation and control of mortgage [3] markets and access to owner-occupation among younger households", *OECD Social, Employment and Migration Working Papers*, No. 196, OECD Publishing, Paris, https://dx.doi.org/10.1787/e16ab00e-en.

World Health Organisation (WHO) (2018), *Global Status Report on Road Safety*, WHO, [21] https://www.who.int/violence_injury_prevention/road_safety_status/2018/en/ (accessed on 5 September 2019).

World Health Organization (WHO) (2018), *WHO Housing and Health Guidelines*, [10] https://www.who.int/sustainable-development/publications/housing-health-guidelines/en/ (accessed on 17 June 2019).

Notes

1 Governments identify groups at risk of housing exclusion differently. For instance, in the United States, some groups (determined by colour, disability, familial status, national origin, race or ethnicity, religion or gender) are legally protected from housing discrimination, as defined in the Fair Housing Act. Other countries identify specific target groups to be supported by housing policies: female head of households, people who have been displaced or lost their homes due to natural disasters (Brazil); people with disabilities, seniors, victims of domestic violence, indigenous communities (Canada); people living in extreme poverty, people who have been displaced, including by national disasters, people living in areas at risk (Colombia); victims of gender violence or victims of terrorism (Spain); low-income households, the homeless, seniors, and households with children (Germany); young families (Lithuania); people with disabilities, seniors, the homeless (Luxembourg); victims of natural disasters, low-income households, seniors, people with disabilities, people caring for others, among others (Latvia); low- and moderate-income households (Poland); low-income households, young people, seniors, victims of domestic violence, the homeless (Portugal) (based on country responses to the 2019 OECD Questionnaire on Affordable and Social Housing, QuASH)).

2 Please refer to (OECD, 2019[7]) for further details on the consumption estimates cited in this report.

3 Austria, Belgium, the Czech Republic, Finland, Germany, Greece, Hungary, Ireland, Latvia, Lithuania, Luxembourg, the Netherlands, Norway, Poland, Portugal, the Slovak Republic, Slovenia, Spain, Sweden and Turkey.

4 Austria, Belgium, Finland, Germany, Greece, Ireland, Luxembourg, the Netherlands, Portugal and Sweden.

5 There are significant cross-national differences in housing spending trends among households. Since 2005, the share of household spending on housing has increased in all OECD countries for which estimates are available, yet the pace of the increase varies considerably across countries. This points to differences in how the global economic crisis affected housing consumption in different countries, and that national policies make a difference. It is also important to note that country averages hide huge within-country differences in levels of household spending on housing, as well as in their evolution over time, which have significant effects on the impact of housing on inequality. More research is needed to understand the drivers of these differences across and within countries.

6 Housing costs can refer to: i) a narrow definition based on rent and mortgage costs (principal repayment and mortgage interest); or ii) a wider definition that also includes costs of mandatory services and charges, regular maintenance and repair, taxes and utilities, also referred to as "total housing costs."

7 Austria, Belgium, the Czech Republic, Finland, Germany, Greece, Hungary, Ireland, Latvia, Lithuania, Luxembourg, the Netherlands, Norway, Poland, Portugal, the Slovak Republic, Slovenia, Spain, Sweden and Turkey.

8 Austria, Belgium, Finland, Germany, Greece, Ireland, Luxembourg, the Netherlands, Portugal and Sweden.

9 The authors define higher opportunity neighbourhoods as a commuting zone or county in which the children whose families are already living in the neighbourhood (e.g. sitting residents) have higher average incomes as adults (Chetty et al., 2015[71]).

10 Australia, Brazil, Canada, Denmark, France, Ireland, Mexico, the Netherlands, New Zealand, South Africa, the United Kingdom, the United States.

11 The net migration rate is the difference between the number of immigrants and the number of emigrants (people leaving an area).

12 The survey, conducted for the first time in two waves in the spring and autumn of 2018, draws on a representative sample of 22 000 people aged 18 to 70 years old in 21 OECD countries: Austria, Belgium, Canada, Chile, Denmark, Estonia, Finland, France, Germany, Greece, Israel, Ireland, Italy, Lithuania, Mexico, the Netherlands, Norway, Poland, Portugal, Slovenia and the United States. Respondents are asked about their social and economic concerns, how well they think government responds to their needs and expectations, and what policies they would like to see in the future.

13 This estimate excludes individuals living in homes that are owned outright (i.e. there is no longer a mortgage to pay off) in order to better assess the share of individuals who, among those who have something to pay for housing, pay more than 40% of their disposable income.

14 One study from the United States found that the presence of safety and accessibility features reduced the likelihood of a serious fall among the elderly by 20 percentage points; in addition, estimates suggested that investments in home safety and accessibility features in housing were largely offset by a nearly equal reduction in medical costs (Eriksen, Greenhalgh-Stanley and Engelhardt, 2015[70]).

15 The OECD Affordable Housing Database (indicators HC3.1 and HC3.2) and the OECD Policy Brief, "Better data and policies to fight homelessness in the OECD" (OECD, 2020[61]) document recent cross-national trends in homelessness and discuss the data and definitional constraints in measuring homelessness across countries.

16 There is no internationally agreed upon definition of homelessness, and countries do not define or count the homeless in the same way. Authorities may use administrative data (such as registries from shelters and local authorities), point-in-time estimates (such as street counts, which are often conducted annually at a given time of year), or a combination of both. Both methods provide only a partial picture of homelessness, and neither effectively captures the "hidden homeless" – people who may not be visibly homeless or appear in official statistics, either because they do not seek formal support or they seek shelter with family or friends, or live in their car. Definitional differences drive some of the variation in the reported incidence of homelessness across countries; these differences hamper international comparison and an understanding of the differences in homelessness rates and risks across countries. There are also a number of challenges in the scope, frequency, consistency and methods of data collection that might affect measuring the full extent of homelessness. For further details, refer to indicators HC3.1 and HC3.2 in (OECD, 2019[6]) and (OECD, 2020[61]).

3 How can housing policies and governance help deliver inclusive growth?

This section assesses the housing policy response in OECD countries and proposes a series of policy considerations to support more inclusive housing outcomes. A first series of considerations are more structural, aiming to boost the supply of affordable housing and address some of the distortions in the housing market that have an impact on inclusion and affordability. The second set aims to improve the housing outcomes and opportunities of low-income households, children, youth, seniors and the homeless.

It is clear from the previous sections that housing matters for inclusive growth, and that some populations face important barriers in the housing market. This section explores a range of considerations to ensure that housing policies and governance can help foster more inclusive growth. As summarised in Table 3.1, a first set of considerations aims to address the structural barriers to expanding the supply of affordable housing as well as some of the distortions in the housing market that have an impact on inclusion and affordability. The second set aims to improve the housing outcomes and opportunities of low-income households, children, youth, seniors and the homeless.

Housing policy and governance are complex, and solutions must be tailored to country contexts and challenges. There is no single measure or approach that will ensure that housing policies deliver more inclusive growth: rather, it will take a range of coordinated actions at different levels of government to foster more equitable housing outcomes and opportunities, and make stable, quality housing accessible to more people.

3.1. Rethinking housing policies and governance to deliver inclusive growth

Governments could begin by addressing some of the structural barriers to inclusive growth in the housing market through efforts to boost the overall supply of affordable housing and address distortions in the housing market. Such efforts could go a long way to levelling the playing field across different actors and tenure types, which could generate benefits to all households, including the most vulnerable.

3.1.1. Make housing an integral part of an inclusive growth strategy

Housing should be a key feature of an inclusive growth strategy, and central to a government's efforts to "invest in people and places that have been left behind," as outlined in the *OECD Framework for Policy Action on Inclusive Growth* (OECD, 2018[1]). As discussed in the previous sections, housing and the neighbourhood in which people live matter for individual outcomes, and their access to opportunity to improve their life chances. It is also a key building block that can help sustain and more equitably share the gains of economic growth (OECD, 2018[1]).

To ensure that housing can help deliver inclusive growth, a whole-of-government approach is needed. This is because in many OECD countries, housing policy making is fragmented across ministries and levels of government. This diversity is, on the one hand, a reflection of the many implications of housing on both individuals and the economy. On the other hand, fragmentation in housing policy making can contribute to higher levels of inequality in support for affordable housing and the delivery of public services: the range of actors involved makes it more likely that some individuals or groups "fall through the cracks" of public support (Dewilde and De Decker, 2016[2]).

Only a minority of OECD countries have a dedicated housing ministry (Table 3.2). The lead housing ministry for housing varies widely across countries, and may fall under the authority of ministries of Economy, Finance, Development, Environment or Social Affairs (OECD, 2019[3]). In many countries, housing policies are further fragmented across a range of ministries, as different aspects of housing policy fall under the authority of different ministries. For instance, housing-related taxation may be handled by the Ministry of Finance; energy efficiency regulations by the Ministry of Environment; and issues relating to housing benefits, homelessness by the Ministry of Social Welfare. This is the case in Austria, where four ministries have authority for different dimensions of housing policy (the Ministry of Digital and Economic Affairs; the Ministry for Constitutional Affairs, Reforms, Deregulation and Justice; the Ministry of Finance; and, the Ministry for Sustainability and Tourism), and in the Czech Republic (the Ministry of Labour and Social Affairs; the Ministry of the Interior; the Ministry of Finance; and, the Ministry of Environment) (OECD, 2019[3]).

Table 3.1. Housing policy considerations for more inclusive growth

Policy objective(s)	Potential measures to consider
Addressing structural barriers to boost the supply of affordable housing and help deliver inclusive growth	
Make housing an integral part of an Inclusive Growth strategy	• Given the fragmentation of housing governance across ministries and levels of government, pursue a whole-of-government approach to housing policy that prioritises inclusive growth; • Coordinate housing with other key policy domains and services, such as health and transport, to ensure that vulnerable groups do not fall through the cracks of social support systems.
Expand the supply of affordable and social housing so that more people can access good quality dwellings	• Consider reforms to local planning, land-use and zoning regulations; • Review fiscal frameworks that may influence (largely local) housing and urban development decisions; • Invest in social and/or affordable housing construction, through direct investments and/or subsidies and other financial support to developers; • Facilitate advances in housing construction technology, building materials and processes to drive down construction costs.
Apply an inclusive lens to the overall housing policy approach	• Phase out some of the tax advantages that favour home ownership and typically benefit higher-income households, which can also hamper the pursuit of other key policy objectives to promote inclusive growth, such as related to labour mobility.
Improve housing and neighbourhood quality to boost individuals' access to opportunity	• Provide financial support to individual households and/or landlords (in the case of rental housing) to improve housing quality; • Invest in urban renewal strategies to improve neighbourhood quality, boost the overall accessibility to jobs and services, and reduce spatial segregation.

Make the private rental market more affordable	• Strike a better balance in tenancy regulations in the private rental market between landlord and tenant rights, which could include:
	  o Introducing controls of rent increases (e.g. rent stabilisation measures) within and/or across tenancies, where relevant;
	  o Increasing transparency and enforcement of rental regulations to address problems when tenants and/or landlords breach their rental contact, which facilitates greater security for landlords and increased quality and security of tenure for tenants.

Overcoming the specific housing challenges facing low-income households, children, youth, seniors and the homeless	
Improve targeting of public support for housing to ensure it benefits those who need it most	• Invest more in social housing, mindful of considerations of social mixing.
Help youth and families with children get on a stable, affordable housing ladder	• Expand existing supports for young people in the private rental market, social housing and co-operative living arrangements to help youth get on a stable, quality housing ladder (beyond home ownership). *To improve access to home ownership:* • Refine first-time homeowner programmes to better target households in greatest need; • Explore different home ownership models, including shared equity and shared ownership models; • Develop programmes to enable workers on temporary/non-traditional employment contracts to be eligible to apply for a mortgage.
Help elderly households meet their evolving housing needs and combat ageing unequally	• Help elderly households meet their evolving housing needs by investing in tailored improvements to housing quality and accessibility (e.g. through tax relief, subsidies and/or grants) that can support individual preferences to age in place for as long as feasible; • Explore the potential for co-operative living arrangements that bring together youth and seniors.
Invest in homelessness prevention and provide targeted support to the homeless	• Support homelessness prevention by investing in affordable housing; • Tailor support to the diverse needs of the homeless population; • Develop broad-based support for homelessness strategies, which are underpinned by co-operation among authorities at different levels of government and non-public actors; • Improve data collection of homelessness to better understand the challenges and needs of different homeless populations.

In addition, housing competencies and decisions that have critical implications for housing, such as land use planning and zoning regulations, are typically spread out across different levels of government. While housing tax relief measures are often designed and administered at national level, many aspects of land use regulations and the administration of property taxes are the competency of subnational authorities (OECD, 2017[4]). Social housing responsibilities can also be spread across levels of government, where funding decisions may be in the hands of national government, but the management and allocation of social housing handled at subnational level (Phillips, 2020[5]).

As a result of the fragmentation of housing policies across ministries and levels of government, housing objectives in one ministry (or level of government) may be at odds with those in other policy domains (or levels of government). For instance, nationally designed public support for affordable housing development frequently runs into local planning processes that block the construction of new affordable housing (OECD, 2017[4]).

There is thus scope to improve the interaction between housing policies with other key dimensions of inclusive growth to ensure that inclusion concerns are central to housing decisions. A more co-ordinated discharge of housing policy with operations and investments in other areas, such as health and education, can facilitate the development of quality neighbourhoods, in which new housing is also well connected to transport, jobs, quality schools and health services (OECD, 2015[6]; 2015[7]). This is important for all households, but especially for children, for whom quality neighbourhoods are central to their development and future prospects.

Table 3.2. The lead housing ministry varies considerably across countries

Lead ministry at national level responsible for housing policies, as reported in the 2019 OECD QuASH

Lead ministry for housing policies	Countries
Ministry of Economy and/or Finance	Estonia, Italy, Latvia, Sweden
Ministry of Interior	Germany[1], the Netherlands
Housing/Urban Development	Canada[2], Chile, Colombia, Costa Rica, Denmark, Ireland, Luxembourg, Mexico, New Zealand, Portugal, Switzerland, Turkey, England (United Kingdom), United States
Environment	Finland
Regional Development/Territorial cohesion/Local government	Bulgaria, Brazil, the Czech Republic, France, Norway, Romania
Economic Development/Infrastructure	Spain[3], Japan[4,] Korea[5], Poland, the Slovak Republic[6]
Social Affairs	Iceland, Malta
Shared across ministries	Australia, Austria
No lead ministry	Greece
Not a direct national competency; handled at subnational level	Belgium

Note: For some countries, the competencies of the ministry reported as lead for housing may fall into multiple categories of this table; in these cases, the name of the ministry is reported in the notes that follow. (1) Germany: Ministry of Interior and Building. (2) Canada: Canada Mortgage and Housing Corporation. (3) Spain: Ministry of Development. (4) Japan: Ministry of Land, Infrastructure, Transport and Tourism. (5) Korea: Ministry of Land, Infrastructure and Transport. (6) Slovak Republic: Ministry of Transport and Construction.
Source: OECD Affordable Housing Database (http://oe.cd/ahd), Indicator PH1.1. Drawing on country responses to the OECD Questionnaire on Affordable and Social Housing (QuASH).

3.1.2. Expand the supply of social and affordable housing so that more people can access good quality dwellings

Boosting housing affordability and stimulating the overall supply of (affordable) housing is identified as a top housing policy objective for many OECD countries (OECD, 2019[3]). But governments could do more to boost the supply of affordable housing, which could generate significant gains for vulnerable households. Many OECD countries face obstacles to expand the supply of affordable housing, albeit with very different country contexts. Since 2000, overall investment (both public and private) in housing[1] has been uneven across the OECD. On average in OECD countries, direct investment (gross fixed capital formation) in housing grew significantly prior to the financial crisis, before dropping sharply around 2007 and then increasing steadily from around 2013, but trends vary considerably across countries (Annex C).

Meanwhile, public investment (public capital expenditure) in dwellings has more than halved since 2001 across the OECD on average (Figure 3.1). Over the past two decades, government spending on capital transfers and gross capital formation for "housing development"[2] has dropped from around 0.17% of GDP on average across the OECD to about 0.07% of GDP in 2018. In particular, direct investment in dwellings has faded away since the Global Financial Crisis, amounting to less than 0.01% of GDP in 2018. Meanwhile, the volume of capital transfers, which makes up the bulk of public investment on housing, has fallen to a lesser extent. Nevertheless, at less than 0.1% of GDP on average since the Global Financial crisis, public investment in dwellings is not high. By comparison, demand-side housing assistance, measured in terms of public expenditure on housing allowances, has risen slightly over the same period, from 0.26% of GDP in 2001 to 0.31% GDP in 2017. Meanwhile, the share of social housing has declined in most OECD countries since 2010, further reducing the affordable housing supply for low-income households (OECD, forthcoming[8]).

Figure 3.1. Public investment in dwellings has fallen, while spending on housing allowances is holding up

Public capital transfers and public direct investment in housing development, and public spending on housing allowances and rent subsidies, OECD-25 average, as percentage GDP, 2001 to 2018

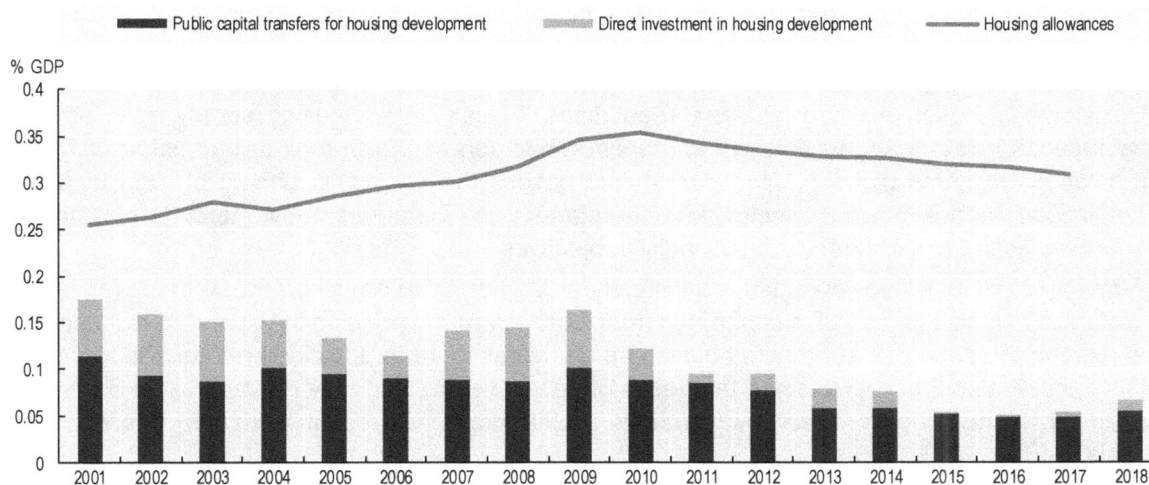

Note: The OECD-25 average is the unweighted average across the 25 OECD countries with capital transfer and gross capital formation data available from 2001. It excludes Australia, Canada, Chile, Iceland, Israel, Japan, Korea, Lithuania, New Zealand, Turkey and the United States. Direct investment in housing development (COFOG series P5_K2CG) refers to government gross capital formation in housing development. Public capital transfers for housing development (COFOG series D9CG) refers to indirect capital expenditure made through transfers to organisations outside of government. Housing development includes, among other things, the acquisition of land needed for the construction of dwellings, the construction or purchase and remodelling of dwelling units for the general public or for people with special needs, and grants or loans to support the expansion, improvement or maintenance of the housing stock. See the Eurostat Manual on sources and methods for the compilation of COFOG Statistics (https://ec.europa.eu/eurostat/documents/3859598/5917333/KS-RA-11-013-EN.PDF) for more detail. Spending on housing allowances does not include spending on mortgage relief, capital subsidies towards construction and implicit subsidies towards accommodation costs.
Source: (OECD, 2019[9]) – Indicator PH1.1, drawing on data from the OECD National Accounts Database, www.oecd.org/sdd/na/, and provisional data from OECD Social Expenditure Database, www.oecd.org/social/expenditure.htm.

The shortfall in investment has contributed to housing supply failing to keep pace with housing demand. There are nevertheless significant regional differences within countries: job-rich urban centres tend to experience housing shortages, while declining areas may face an oversupply of housing (e.g. a large share of vacant houses). In addition, many countries are experiencing shortages specifically in the affordable and/or rental housing stock.[3]

A number of factors have constrained the development of the housing supply. These include, *inter alia*, increasing construction costs, labour shortages, high land prices and/or land scarcity, overly restrictive land regulations and planning processes, among others. Expanding the affordable and rental housing sectors in particular may face further challenges, such as financing gaps and opposition from local residents. Investments in the rental stock may be discouraged by public policies – particularly housing taxation – that tend to benefit owner-occupied dwellings over rental dwellings (discussed further below), or tenancy regulations that are overly protective of tenants. Finally, the specific historical context in some Eastern European countries has led to highly unbalanced tenure arrangements, which are dominated by homeowners with a very small (formal) private rental market (see, for instance, a discussion of the case of Latvia, in OECD (2020[10])).

As a result, there is scope to boost investment in the affordable housing supply. Several avenues could be worth considering:

- In places where prices are high and supply growth is low, reforms to local planning, land-use and zoning regulations may be warranted, as they may place an outsized burden on new housing development (OECD, 2017[4]). Restrictions on development through zoning and building height regulations, for instance, have been shown to drive up housing prices (Glaeser and Gyourko, 2002[11]; 2003[12]; Glaeser, Gyourko and Saks, 2005[13]). In lower-density jurisdictions facing affordability challenges, increased flexibility in local planning and development regulations (e.g. permission to develop at higher densities and/or to allow for smaller units, such as "in-law" or accessory dwelling units; as well as reduced parking requirements; etc.) could help boost supply. Decisions to loosen existing land-use regulations to encourage housing supply must also be balanced against measures that aim to prevent urban sprawl, which may call for tighter land use regulations in some places. Authorities should assess the net public benefit of local land use regulations in the housing sector to understand how measures may support, or impede, affordability and environmental sustainability objectives.

- A review of fiscal frameworks that may influence (largely local) housing and urban development decisions can also be useful to identify whether local governments have the appropriate incentives to expand the supply of affordable housing. In some cases, municipalities are required to pay for the costs of infrastructure to cover the needs of new residents, but may not receive an equivalent share of tax revenue from the new residents (or via intergovernmental transfers) to cover such costs (OECD, 2017[4]).

- Governments could also invest further in social and affordable housing (Box 3.1). In addition, governments could also provide subsidies and other financial support to developers to incentivise affordable housing construction. As summarised in OECD (2019[3]), 24 countries offer support to developers to finance affordable housing; such support can be in the form of tax relief or tax credits, grants, subsidised land or other support.

- To mitigate rising construction costs, advances in housing construction technology, building materials and processes (such as 3-D printing of houses that will be piloted in the Netherlands (Boffey, 2018[14])) also hold promise to drive down construction costs and facilitate more rapid housing construction. Governments can look for ways to support such innovations, as well as consider whether changes in existing regulations are needed.

  Investments in housing construction should be co-ordinated with related investments in transport and other key infrastructure to ensure quality neighbourhoods that are accessible to employment centres. A narrow focus on housing construction that fails to take into account the infrastructure and accessibility dimensions of such urban developments can prove problematic (see, for instance, (OECD, 2015[7])).

Box 3.1. Social housing can be a key part of the affordable housing solution.

Social housing is an important dimension of social welfare policy and affordable housing provision, representing more than 27 million dwellings and about 7% of the total housing stock in OECD and EU countries. Social housing is defined as residential rental accommodation provided at sub-market prices and allocated according to specific rules, such as waiting lists or hardship categories (Salvi del Pero et al., 2016[15]). Yet there are significant differences across countries in the definition, size, scope, target population and type of provider of social housing. For instance, social rental housing makes up less than 10% of the total dwelling stock in most OECD and EU countries, but more than 20% of the total stock in Austria, Denmark and the Netherlands, where it represents a key "third sector" in the housing market. In addition, the social housing sector has been shrinking in recent years in all but six countries for which data are available, due in part to a decline in public investment in the housing stock.

Investments in social housing construction and renovation can be a central part of a more sustainable, inclusive economic recovery as countries chart the path towards economic recovery in the wake of COVID-19. Indeed, policy makers and housing advocates in Australia, Ireland, Portugal, the United Kingdom (England), among others, have emphasised the need to prioritise social and affordable housing as a key counter-cyclical investment opportunity that can help support jobs and SMEs in the building sector and deliver more affordable housing in the market. At the same time, large-scale investment in social housing renovation and refurbishment, which is central element of the European Green Deal and the "Renovation Wave" announced in early 2020, can stimulate economic recovery, support environmental sustainability objectives and boost well-being among residents across the OECD and EU.

Source: (OECD, forthcoming[8]).

3.1.3. Apply an inclusive lens to the overall housing policy approach

Governments have a mix of tools to intervene in the housing market. These may include demand-side housing support to individuals and households (e.g. housing allowances, subsidies for potential homebuyers), as well as supply-side interventions that aim to stimulate (affordable) housing construction (e.g. subsidies and incentives to housing developers) (OECD, 2019[3]). Country responses to the 2019 OECD Questionnaire on Affordable and Social Housing (QuASH), as summarised in Box 3.2, suggest that while housing support for low-income households is available in most countries, the majority of housing policies in the OECD tend to be skewed towards home ownership (Andrews and Sánchez, 2011[16]; André, 2010[17]; Salvi del Pero et al., 2016[15]). Meanwhile, support for tenants in the private rental market is, on average, more piecemeal across OECD countries. While there are many arguments in favour of home ownership, such advantages do not always support inclusion objectives (Box 3.3).

Housing taxation is one of the more powerful policy tools and has resulted in a system that "is far from neutral" in terms of housing tenure, as owner-occupied housing tends to be taxed at lower rates than those who have purchased housing and rent it out (André, 2010[17]; Brys et al., forthcoming[18]) (OECD, 2018[19]). The tax advantages to homeowners can accrue in several ways:

- First, the vast majority of OECD countries tax rental income, but most do not tax imputed rents for homeowners (Denmark, Greece, the Netherlands and Switzerland are the exceptions, although this is generally at low rates) (Brys et al., forthcoming[18]). To some extent, property taxes replace taxes on imputed income in many countries, but revenue from property taxes tends to be low and they are commonly based on outdated property values. Property taxes are also to some extent de facto fees for local services as opposed to taxes on the imputed rental income from housing. In addition, if flat rates apply, property taxes may have less scope than income taxes to be progressive, and less scope to redistribute, particularly if levied at the local level.

- Second, tax relief for mortgage interest provides a significant advantage to debt-financing homeowners in many OECD countries, allowing homeowners to deduct mortgage interest payments from their personal income tax. The benefit provided by mortgage interest relief tends to outweigh the combined effect of all other taxes levied on a debt-financed housing investment (Brys et al., forthcoming[18]).

- Third, owner-occupied dwellings are often exempted from taxes on capital gains, while this is typically not the case for capital gains on rental housing (André, 2010[17]).

- As a result, countries effectively subsidise home ownership through their tax system – meaning that the tax credits and deductions available to homeowners are higher than the taxes that are levied on the dwelling over its lifetime. Because high-income and high-wealth households tend to own a larger share of housing assets relative to lower-income households (in terms of more expensive primary residences as well as investments in secondary residences), they accrue even greater benefits from housing taxation policies that provide disproportionate advantages to homeowners (Brys et al., forthcoming[18]). In addition, policy such as tax relief for mortgage interest often provides larger benefits to taxpayers at higher income brackets who own larger homes and are taxed at higher marginal rates.

Tax relief for home ownership can mean significant savings for homeowners, but the longer term benefits are unclear. Overall, the case for tax relief for housing investment (including mortgage interest relief) is weaker in countries that do not tax imputed income: why should governments subsidise the cost of housing if they are not taxing the income? And while one-off tax relief for first-time home buyers can provide targeted support to young households entering the property market for the first time, it can also drive up house prices (Berry, 2003[20]).

As a result, governments could better support affordability and inclusion objectives by taking a more balanced approach to housing tenure, notably through reforms to housing taxation. A careful assessment of the design and implementation of the existing policy instruments in each country would be necessary to identify the most potentially effective reforms. However, one key area to explore is the phasing out of some of the tax advantages that favour home ownership and tend to benefit higher-income groups. Eliminating (or capping, or conversion into a tax credit so as to provide the same benefit to high- and low-income earners) mortgage interest rate deductibility, for instance, can help make housing taxation more progressive (Causa and Woloszko, 2019[21]). Taxing capital gains, especially on residences other than the primary residence, and rates closer to the rates of incomes taxes could also support equity in housing taxation. A broad-based tax concerning all residential property with higher rates on more valuable property and/or higher rates on second or third properties would have positive outcomes for efficiency and equity. For further discussion of housing taxation policies, see Brys et al. (forthcoming[18]; forthcoming[22]).

Box 3.2. Summary of country responses to the 2019 OECD Questionnaire on Affordable and Social Housing (QuASH)

Country responses[1] to the 2019 OECD QuASH as summarised in Figure 3.2 and further detailed in the OECD Affordable Housing Database (OECD, 2019[3]), provide insights into the scope, design and implementation of housing policy interventions prior to the COVID-19 pandemic. Emergency housing support introduced by governments during the COVID-19 pandemic is discussed at the end of this chapter, and in OECD (2020[23]) and OECD (2020[24]).

Figure 3.2. The majority of countries have housing allowances, social housing and financial support for home ownership.

Overview of housing policy instruments prior to COVID-19: Number of reporting countries adopting each policy type

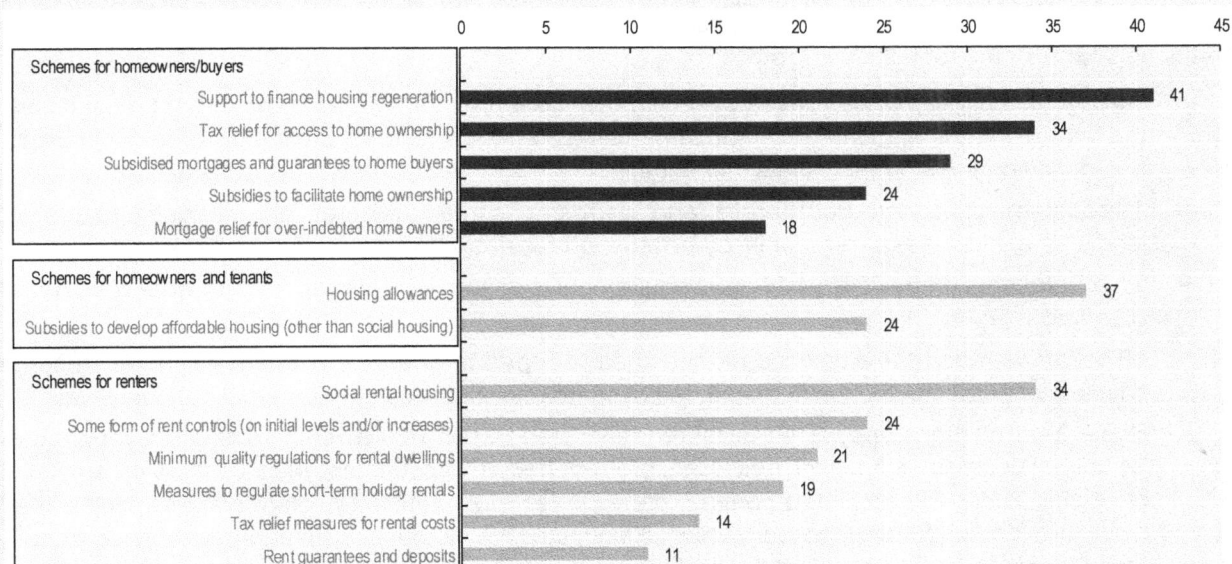

Note: 1. Not all countries responded to all sections of the QuASH. 2. Limited information was provided for Croatia, Cyprus, Greece, Hungary, Korea, Romania, Slovenia, South Africa and Turkey.
Source: OECD Affordable Housing Database (http://oe.cd/ahd), Indicator PH1.1. Based on country responses to the 2019 and 2016 OECD QuASH.

Housing allowances (also known as housing benefits or vouchers) and subsidised (social) housing are two of the most common forms of *housing support for low-income households*:

- 37 countries provide *housing allowances* (also known as housing benefits or vouchers) in the form of cash transfers earmarked to support housing costs. The vast majority of housing allowances are means-tested, although the income threshold varies considerably across countries.
- *Subsidised (social) rental housing* exists in 34 countries. Governments may support the subsidised rental housing supply through direct provision of social housing, or by supporting the sector through grants, tax credits, loans and/or loan guarantees to social housing providers. The majority, but not all, of social housing programmes are means-tested, though income thresholds may be more or less restrictive, depending on the country (for further discussion, see (OECD, 2020[25]).

However, most housing measures are designed to *support prospective or existing homeowners*:

- 34 countries offer *tax relief for homeowners*, most often in the form of one-off tax relief for buying a home, tax relief for mortgage payments, or tax deductions on mortgage interest payments.

- 24 countries provide *subsidies to households to facilitate home ownership*, often in the form of grants or loans to first-time homebuyers. Some countries offer more than three types of subsidies to households (e.g. Australia, Brazil, Chile, Colombia, Ireland, Mexico, South Africa and Spain).

- 29 countries offer *mortgage support to households*, most often in the form of subsidised mortgages or mortgage guarantees.

- 41 countries offer *support to finance housing regeneration* – that is, improvements to the quality of existing dwellings, which may include energy efficiency upgrades.

- 18 countries offer *mortgage relief to homeowners in financial distress*.

Public support towards **the private rental market** is much more piecemeal across countries, spanning tax relief, rent guarantees or deposits, and regulations (at national, regional or local level). Some measures (e.g. rent control) may not be uniformly applied within a country, but rather only in certain jurisdictions and/or segments of the rental housing stock:

- 14 countries offer *tax relief measures of rental costs for individual taxpayers*; in most cases, the tax relief is for landlords of rental properties as a means to boost the supply of rental housing, though in some countries tenants can benefit.

- 11 countries offer *rent guarantees and deposits*; some measures are designed to protect landlords against loss of rent, while others support tenants who cannot afford initial rental deposits.

- 21 countries report that there is a legal requirement to ensure a *minimum level of quality of rental dwellings*.

- 19 countries report the existence of measures to *regulate short-term holiday rentals*; in some cases, measures have been implemented by large municipalities rather than at national level.

- Some form of *rent controls* on initial rent levels and/or on rent level increases are reported in 24 countries (controls on initial rent levels are reported in 13 countries, while controls on rent level increases during the term of a contract are reported in 22 countries). Rent controls, where they exist, are not uniformly applied within all countries, in some places applying only to certain jurisdictions and/or segments of the rental housing stock.

- There is considerable variation across countries in the *minimum duration of rental agreements*. In 26 countries, the duration of the rental contract can be freely negotiated between the landlord and the tenant. Many countries nonetheless impose a minimum duration of the rental contract (for instance, a minimum of three years in Austria, Costa Rica and Norway), but there is little consistency across countries in the minimum duration.

- In most OECD countries, *tenancy regulation* in the private rental market is governed by the national government; in a handful of countries (Australia, Belgium and Canada), it is a regional competency, while in others it is shared across levels of government (Iceland and the United States).

Note: 1. The 2019 QuASH was circulated to nearly 50 countries, including OECD countries, non-OECD countries in the European Union, and Key Partners/Accession countries. Not all countries responded to all sections of the QuASH, thus the number of reporting countries varies across policy instruments.
Source: Country responses to the 2019 OECD Questionnaire on Affordable and Social Housing (QuASH).

Box 3.3. Should public policies give preference to home ownership?

There are many arguments in favour of home ownership, such as i) wealth accumulation, ii) child outcomes, iii) social capital and iv) mobility (Andrews and Caldera Sánchez, 2011[26]). For instance, home ownership has been considered a vehicle for asset and wealth accumulation, but changes to mortgage financing in recent years have weakened such effects. Home ownership can play an important role in maintaining standards of living of retired households. It has also been linked to higher test scores and better behaviour among children (perhaps reflecting the increased geographic stability that may come with home ownership). Home ownership has been linked to higher levels of residential stability and more active and informed citizens relative to renters (measured *inter alia* by higher voter turnout), yet other studies have not found strong links between home ownership and civic engagement.

Nevertheless, the policy preference towards home ownership does not always support inclusion. Andrews and Caldera Sánchez (2011[16]) argue that "the case for subsidising home ownership is far from clear," and empirical evidence does not consensually support the causal links between home ownership and a range of positive spillovers for society (Causa and Woloszko, 2019[21]). Home ownership support, in some cases, undermines affordability and inclusion objectives, in that it can:

- *Make it harder for low-income and young households to become homeowners*: Outsized support towards home ownership creates distortions in the housing market and can increase house price volatility (André, 2010[17]), making it harder for lower-income and younger households to become homeowners. Tax advantages can increase demand for housing, which can lead to an increase in house prices. In countries with tight housing supply, the tax subsidy can be largely capitalised into housing prices, reducing housing affordability overall and redistributing income from (potentially younger) first-time homebuyers to (potentially older) existing homeowners, with the potential to exacerbate intergenerational inequality (André, 2010[17]; Andrews and Sánchez, 2011[16]).

- *Fail to reach households who most need support*: Home ownership support does not always reach households in greatest need – nor, as evidence from Denmark has shown, does it necessarily lead to a higher incidence of home ownership (Gruber, Jensen and Kleven, 2017[27]). Country experiences illustrate that subsidies to first-time homebuyers can – inadvertently or by design – ultimately provide support to people who would have been able to purchase a home *without* the subsidy; rather, the subsidy enables some households to purchase bigger or higher quality homes.[4] This challenge is particularly relevant for home ownership support measures that are not means-tested (Salvi del Pero et al., 2016[15]).

- *Impede residential and labour mobility*: Home ownership may also have a negative impact on social and labour mobility, by discouraging people to relocate and benefit from new economic opportunities (Causa and Woloszko, 2019[21]; Andrews and Sánchez, 2011[16]). High property transaction taxes exacerbate the negative effect of home ownership, and transaction costs can vary significantly by region or even by type of household.

- *Crowd out other types of housing support*: Home ownership support is, in most countries, expensive. Even if such support can generate the desired outcomes, policies to encourage home ownership account for a significant share of government spending on housing in many OECD countries. It may be possible to achieve similar positive effects more efficiently through other policies.

The design and selection of different types of housing support should also take into account the potential impacts on residential and labour mobility. This is because housing can facilitate, or impede, households' ability to move homes, and by extension, enable workers to match their skills to available employment opportunities (Box 3.4). Obstacles to residential mobility, in turn, affect labour mobility by creating inefficiencies in the labour market that impede workers from relocating to a job that best matches their skills (OECD, 2011[28]; Sánchez and Andrews, 2011[29]; Sánchez and Andrews, 2011[30]; Oswald, 2009[31]).

Box 3.4. Housing and residential mobility

Housing has important implications for residential and labour mobility. Housing can facilitate, or impede, households' ability to move homes, and by extension, enable workers to match their skills to available employment opportunities. Housing type and tenure matter, as do other aspects of the housing market – such as large regional housing price differences that make it more costly for households to move. Research suggests:

- Homeowners tend to be less mobile than renters, because they face higher transaction cost to move residences and thus tend to move less often (Oswald, 1996[32]; Oswald, 2009[31]; OECD, 2011[28]; Sánchez and Andrews, 2011[29]; Sánchez and Andrews, 2011[30]; Causa and Pichelmann, forthcoming 2020[33]).

- Residential mobility is lower among households receiving a subsidy or paying below-market rents, as compared to private tenants in most countries. This may be because social housing tenants would be reluctant to give up below-market rent and relatively secure tenancy, and would face difficulties in quickly securing a spot in social housing in another jurisdiction (Causa and Pichelmann, forthcoming 2020[33]).

- However, public spending on housing allowances and total social spending on housing are significantly *positively* associated with mobility. This may suggest that public support for low-income households, both cash and in-kind, encourages mobility by making moving more affordable, provided that social housing is designed to discourage lock-in effects that impede mobility (for example, by waiving residency or queuing requirements in the case of unemployed workers taking up a job in the region) (Causa and Pichelmann, forthcoming 2020[33]).

- Housing allowances have been shown to have smaller effects on residential mobility, particularly if they are portable (OECD, 2011[28]; Sánchez and Andrews, 2011[29]; Sánchez and Andrews, 2011[30]).

3.1.4. Improve housing and neighbourhood quality to boost individuals' access to opportunity

Improving housing and neighbourhood conditions could go a long way to support inclusive growth objectives, and especially among households with children. All but one of 41 respondent countries to the 2019 OECD QuASH provide financial support to individual households and/or (in the case of rental housing) property owners to improve dwelling quality (OECD, 2019[3]). Such support is most often in the form of grants or, to a lesser extent, tax relief (tax deductions and/or credits). Some programmes give priority to households with children, such as Chile's Family Heritage Protection Programme D.S.255 (*Programa de Protección del Patrimonio Familiar D.S.255 de 2006*) and Rural Habitability Programme D.S. 10 of 2015 (*Programa de Habitabilidad Rural D.S.10 de 2015*); and Colombia's Dignified House, Dignified Life initiative (*Casa Digna Vida Digna*).

In addition to improvements to dwellings, policy makers should also consider how to upgrade neighbourhood quality. Such improvements tend to require coordinated measures and investments across different policy domains and levels of government, in order to improve the quality of opportunities relating to education, public transport and parks, culture and leisure. Some OECD countries, including Chile, France, Mexico and the United States, have initiated largescale urban regeneration programmes. France's

New National Urban Renewal Programme (*Nouveau Programme National de Renouvellement Urbain*) provides funding to local urban renewal programmes following a specific set of eligibility criteria in more than 200 neighbourhoods throughout the country, with an objective to approve 450 projects in total by the end of 2019 (Agence nationale pour la Rénovation Urbaine (ANRU), 2019[34]). Chile has introduced a number of programmes to support urban renewal efforts, namely the Neighbourhood Improvement initiative (*Recuperación de Barrios*) launched in 2006. The Chilean programme focuses on social housing developments, as well as other neighbourhoods that face problems of social vulnerability and segregation, and aims to address the physical deterioration of buildings, public spaces and urban infrastructure, guided by an action plan drawn up in partnership with the community (OECD, 2015[6]). Such efforts can also be instrumental in reducing spatial segregation.

There are important trade-offs to consider. The risk of resident displacement is a significant concern of urban regeneration projects. In some countries, early urban regeneration projects led to the displacement of low-income and vulnerable residents. Displacement could result prior to the regeneration investments as part of resident relocations, or following the regeneration investment (for instance, as a result of higher prices driven by the improved neighbourhood quality, or in cases where regeneration projects resulted in a smaller number of units). The demolition of some of the worst-quality dwellings can also be polarising for communities. Lessons from OECD countries can prove helpful in addressing such concerns. For instance, France and the United States introduced considerable resident consultation as part of the regeneration process to ensure that resident views and needs are better taken into account (OECD, 2015[6]). Country experience also suggests that regeneration efforts can be more effective when they go beyond housing quality improvements to address other neighbourhood deficiencies in public services, parks or other community facilities, such as Chile's *Recuperación de Barrios* programme (OECD, 2015[6]).

3.1.5. Make the private rental market more affordable

In most OECD countries, public policies to support affordability in the rental market are not straightforward. On the one hand, a more loosely regulated private rental market can put tenants – especially low-income and vulnerable households – at a higher risk of poor quality dwellings, excessive rent increases or unfair evictions. On the other hand, regulations that strongly favour tenants over landlords can ultimately create disincentives to invest in rental housing and drive down the overall rental housing supply. Only a minority of OECD countries offer tax advantages for rental housing, which typically target property owners but are sometimes available for tenants. In addition, tenancy regulation in the rental market can be complex, and may not be universally applied within a country, leading to a patchwork of rules and regulations (Box 3.5). It can be hard to strike a balance in fair rental regulations between both tenants and landlords.

The private rental market is of particular importance to low-income households and youth. Low-income renters face a significant housing cost burden (Figure 2.4); youth are the most likely age group to live in private rental housing – around three out of ten youth in the OECD are renters in the private market. This suggests that renters, and especially vulnerable renters, could benefit from a more affordable rental supply.

As such, reforms to regulations in the private rental market that aim to create a better balance between tenants and landlords are an important area for consideration. Broadly speaking, regulations in the rental market should benefit both landlords *and* tenants: that is, they should provide, one the one hand, a secure investment for landlords and investors and, on the other, secure, good-quality housing for tenants (Whitehead and Williams, 2018[35]). There are different dimensions of rental regulations to consider, including security of tenure, minimum dwelling quality standards, enforcement procedures, and – probably the most contentious – rent controls (Whitehead and Williams, 2018[35]). Research from the United States highlights the role of landlord-tenant regulations – and differences in such regulations across jurisdictions – in contributing to the significant variation in eviction rates (Gromis, 2019[36]).

Discussions around rent control regulations have recently been revived in some jurisdictions across the OECD – particularly but not only in large and dynamic urban areas that have seen housing costs rise, such as Paris (France), New York City (United States), Berlin (Germany), the states of California and Oregon (United States), as well as in the United Kingdom and others. Rent controls can take different forms and have evolved over time, but generally aim to impose restrictions on rent levels and/or rent level increases in the private rental market (Lind, 2001[37]; Whitehead and Williams, 2018[35]). Whitehead and Williams (2018[35]) identify three types of rent controls:

- rent freezes, which impose a below-market rate maximum (or ceiling) on the rent
- control of rent levels between tenancies (e.g. when a new tenant moves in)
- control of rent increases within tenancies (also known as rent stabilisation).

Box 3.5 summarises the different types of rent controls, and outlines their advantages and disadvantages.

Box 3.5. Rethinking rent controls

Rent controls are often seen by tenants and housing advocates as an attractive tool, as they can help contain rent increases. Rent controls can be effective in protecting tenants from rapidly rising rent levels and reducing displacement of vulnerable households, particularly when neighbourhoods gain popularity. Some research has shown rent controls to be effective in protecting sitting tenants by limiting their displacement, which can benefit low-income and elderly households, among others (Diamond, Mcquade and Qian, 2019[38]). Rent controls can also serve as a form of "insurance" to protect households from losing their home if their economic circumstances abruptly change (Chakrabarti, 2019[39]). Finally, rent control regulations are (usually) fairly understandable by both landlords and tenants (Dougherty, 2018[40]).

However, depending on how they are structured, rent controls also have important drawbacks. Some argue that they are a tool that "helps renters today at the expense of renters tomorrow" (Dougherty, 2018[40]). Depending on whether they are applied to all or only a subset of the rental stock, rent control regulations only make housing more affordable for those who live in rent-controlled units – at the expense of those who do not. Importantly, such regulations also create a disincentive for landlords and developers to invest in rental housing: this can both discourage maintenance or upgrades to the existing rental housing stock, as well as decrease the supply of rental housing over the longer term by encouraging landlords to exit the rental market and discouraging others not to enter (Dougherty, 2018[40]; Arnott, 1995[41]; Whitehead and Williams, 2018[35]). For instance, one study found that rent control regulations accelerated gentrification by encouraging landlords to convert existing rental housing into more profitable condominiums (Diamond, Mcquade and Qian, 2019[38]). Because they are not means-tested, rent controls tend to be regressive (Favilukis, Mabille and Stern Stijn Van Nieuwerburgh, 2018[42]), and can generate a misallocation of (affordable) housing since they do not necessarily benefit those households who are in greatest need. It can also reduce residential mobility by locking-in tenants (Andrews and Sánchez, 2011[16]; Causa and Woloszko, 2019[21]). The advantages and disadvantages of different forms of rent control are summarised in Table 3.3.

Table 3.3. Types of rent control regulations, as well as their advantages and disadvantages

Type of rent control	Example of possible mechanisms	Target group(s)	Advantages	Disadvantages
Rent freeze (e.g. rent ceiling)	A cap on rent levels at the time of contract agreement	New tenants	Prevents price- gouging in tight housing markets	Can reduce housing quality in the private rental sector, as landlords do not have incentives to invest in housing maintenance and/or upgrades
			Can lead to a significant	Can reduce overall rental supply as

			drop in rent levels (for the dwellings affected by the rent freeze), if rents cannot be adjusted for inflation and rising housing costs	landlords are incentivised to leave and/or not to enter the private rental market
				Can reduce mobility of tenants
Control of rent levels between tenancies	A cap on the (yearly) increase in rent levels	New tenants	Allows landlords to adjust rent levels for cost increases	Can lower potential rate of return for landlords, especially those with long-term tenants
			Reduces incentives for landlords to underinvest in housing maintenance and upgrades	Can discourage new landlords/investors from entering the private rental market, if other investment opportunities would generate higher returns
			Protects tenants against sudden and significant rent increases	Can reduce mobility of tenants
Control of rent increases within tenancies (e.g. rent stabilisation)	A cap on the increase in rent levels for sitting tenants; can be applied at time of control renewal for fixed-term tenancies or at regular intervals for open-ended tenancies	Sitting tenants only	Allows landlords to adjust rent levels periodically based on market conditions (within limits), providing some security over the long-term rate of return	Can lower potential rate of return for landlords, especially those with long-term tenants
			Reduces turnover in the rental market, which can benefit both landlords and tenants	Can discourage new landlords/investors from entering the private rental market, if other investment opportunities would generate higher returns
			Protects tenants from sudden and significant rent increases	Can reduce mobility of tenants
				In the case of long-term tenancies, may benefit better-off households, rather than new entrants who could potentially benefit more from controlled rental increases

Source: (Terner Center for Housing Innovation, 2018[43]; Diamond, Mcquade and Qian, 2019[38]; Favilukis, Mabille and Stern Stijn Van Nieuwerburgh, 2018[42]; Andrews and Sánchez, 2011[16]; Causa and Woloszko, 2019[21]; World Bank, 2018[44]; Whitehead and Williams, 2018[35]; Dougherty, 2018[40]; Chakrabarti, 2019[39]; Jenkins, 2009[45]).

A more nuanced approach to rental regulations that targets the specific challenges of the rental housing market in a given jurisdiction could be warranted. While rent freezes – known as the "first generation" of rent controls – are rarely introduced today, there has been an increasing trend, at least in Europe, towards rent stabilisation measures, whereby rents within (and sometimes between) tenancies are allowed to increase within a certain range (Whitehead and Williams, 2018[35]). Rent stabilisation measures appear to offer security to both tenants and landlords, and may be a solution to consider in a context of a tight rental market. As Whitehead and Williams (2018[35]) conclude, in parallel to rent stabilisation measures, it is important to ensure that other aspects of rental regulations (e.g. security of tenure, minimum dwelling quality standards and enforcement procedures) provide security for both landlords and tenants. This includes the following considerations:

- Minimum housing quality standards should be established and enforced, while being designed to ensure that they do not inflate housing costs.
- There should be efficient enforcement of rental regulations to address problems when tenants and/or landlords breach their rental contact; increased transparency and better enforcement

facilitates greater security for landlords as well as increased quality and security of tenure for tenants.

- Clear conditions for both a landlord and tenant to terminate a rental contract should be in place. No-fault evictions (by which landlords can evict tenants who have been paying their rent on time and have otherwise met the terms of the rental agreement) should be prevented during a tenancy period, subject to minimum notice periods as outlined in the rental agreement.
- In the case of longer-term or indefinite tenancies, there should be clear exemptions that identify the conditions under which a landlord can repossess a dwelling (e.g. the landlord wishes to live in the dwelling, or to sell or upgrade the dwelling).

The COVID-19 pandemic has intensified the vulnerability of renters in some OECD countries, prompting many governments to introduce emergency support measures (discussed further in Section 3.3).

3.2. Overcoming the specific housing barriers facing low-income households, children, youth and seniors

A second set of considerations focuses on how to overcome the specific housing challenges of low-income households, children, youth and seniors. These measures, which target specific vulnerable groups, could complement some of the more structural recommendations highlighted above.

3.2.1. Improve targeting of public support to ensure it benefits those who need it most

In a context of scarce public resources, policy makers could also consider ways to improve targeting of housing support to households in greatest need of public support. Living costs differ across regions and cities within a country, and much of this variation is due to differences in housing prices. Public policy can help to mitigate these differences in housing prices to support access to affordable housing for targeted groups in different ways. For example, governments can promote access to affordable housing through the tax system, directly provide social or public housing, and/or provide housing benefits and/or vouchers that partially offset differences in living costs. The social assistance systems of countries may also aim to account for differences in housing costs across regions (OECD, 1998[46]). More research is needed to understand the most effective mix of policy instruments to meet the housing needs of low-income households in a given national context.

One strategy is to introduce means-testing more regularly throughout the duration of social housing tenancy, and not just at the time of entry, as a basis for adjusting rent levels of better-off tenants or to encourage them to move out of social housing. While low-income households are most likely to live in social housing across the OECD, middle- and higher-income households continue to live in these dwellings in some countries. On the one hand, such social mixing within social housing can be an explicit policy objective (as has typically been the case in, for example, Austria and Denmark). On the other hand, where the social housing stock is limited, it may be relevant to consider strategies to encourage tenants whose circumstances have improved to move to other forms of tenure to make room for households who are more economically vulnerable. Different tools can help manage resident throughfare, including periodic eligibility reviews, fixed-term tenancies (FTT) and income-dependent rent increases, in addition to more targeted criteria to determine social housing eligibility at the outset (OECD, forthcoming[8]). Short-term financial incentives could also be considered to encourage tenants who earn more to graduate out of publicly supported rentals. In the United States, the Family Self-Sufficiency Program allows assisted households to place earnings increases in escrow; for participants of the programme, rent subsidies are not adjusted for the increased income, and upon completion of a counselling programme, the participants receive their savings.

However, more regular means-testing can be practically and politically difficult to implement, and there are important trade-offs to consider. Depending on the design of such measures, they can act as a disincentive to households to improve their economic situation. In addition, limiting social housing tenants to only the poorest households reduces social mixing, can dampen community building and threaten the financial sustainability of the overall social housing system. By extension, if social housing is spatially concentrated, there is a risk of creating pockets of poverty (Salvi del Pero et al., 2016[15]). Such trade-offs must be carefully balanced against the expected gains from more regular means-testing (OECD, forthcoming[8]).

3.2.2. Help youth and young families get on a stable, affordable housing ladder

Policy makers should also explore how to best provide housing support to young adults and families. Rising house prices and increasing instability in the labour market have put home ownership out of reach for many young adults and families in some OECD countries, resulting in youth living longer with their parents or entering an increasingly congested private rental market.

On the one hand, young households would benefit from housing support that does not explicitly aim to make them homeowners. This is not to say that programmes that aim to boost access to home ownership for youth and young families should be eliminated, but rather that a broader range of housing supports, including those that provide assistance to youth living in other forms of tenure (such as renting in the private market, social housing, co-operative living arrangements, etc.), should be considered. For instance, co-living, which brings young adults and seniors under one roof, has been explored in Japan, Portugal, the Netherlands, among other countries (OECD, 2015[47]). The objective could be to support young households in getting on a stable, quality *housing* ladder – rather than necessarily a *home ownership* ladder.

On the other hand, there is still scope to refine and expand efforts to facilitate home ownership among young households. As mentioned, numerous first-time homebuyer programmes are not effectively targeting households that need public support the most. In addition, introducing and/or expanding alternative homeownership models – including shared equity and shared ownership models, discussed below – could also be considered. Such models currently represent a very small fraction of the housing stock in most OECD countries:

- *Shared equity housing models* can provide a path to home ownership for lower-income households while keeping housing affordable over time by restricting the resale value of the home. The resale price of a shared equity home is calculated based on a formula established in the ground lease or deed (for instance), which puts a cap on the amount of equity that a homeowner is permitted to realise and thereby ensures a level of affordability in the resale price for the next income-tested eligible buyer of that property (Wang et al., 2019[48]). In a study of 4 000 shared equity properties over three decades, Wang et al. (2019[48]) found that such properties were effective in providing a stable form of housing and an affordable path to home ownership for lower-income households, a (modest) opportunity for households to build wealth, and preserving housing affordability for subsequent homebuyers.

- *Shared ownership models* offer a gradual path to home ownership by enabling households to purchase a share of a dwelling (for instance, between 25% and 75% of the home's value, typically from a housing association or NGO), while paying an affordable rent on the remaining share. Dwellers can progressively buy additional shares of the home until they are outright owners. Such programmes are available in the United Kingdom, for instance. However, some legal concerns on the model have been raised, particularly the financial and tenancy implications for dwellers should they fall behind on their rent payments (Peaker, 2013[49]).

In addition, solutions to enable (typically young) workers on temporary employment contracts to access mortgages should also be considered, so that newer generations are not excluded from home ownership. An initiative has been introduced in the Netherlands, for instance, to help temporary and flex-workers access mortgages, by which the mortgage application is based on a prospect statement of an employee's future earnings capacity; almost 20 banks and other mortgage providers and 35 temping agencies participate in the programme (Stichting Perspectiefverklaring, n.d.[50]).

3.2.3. Help elderly households meet their evolving housing needs and combat ageing unequally

Housing considerations for an ageing population are also essential, and will require efforts on multiple fronts. Pursuing measures that support seniors' preference to stay in their own homes for as long as feasible, as well as delivering more tailored institutionalised care, could be considered to meet the diverse and changing needs of seniors. This will require investing in improvements to housing quality and accessibility in order to improve the chances for seniors to stay in their homes for as long as feasible (to "age in place"). Sweden and Germany have both introduced financial support measures to households for accessibility-related improvements to support seniors; in Sweden, grants for home accessibility improvements are provided through municipalities and designed to fully cover the cost of interventions, while in Germany senior households can be reimbursed for such costs up to a certain limit per year (Slaug et al., 2017[51]).

In addition, urban planning, transport and design considerations will be essential to improve overall accessibility of seniors' everyday living environments and daily needs. This includes improving the accessibility of sidewalks and public transport; rethinking access to health care and other essential services; and updating local planning and zoning regulations to enable more adapted and flexible arrangements (OECD, 2015[47]). As mentioned, policy makers could also explore the potential for alternative tenure arrangements, such as co-living that brings young adults and seniors under one roof (OECD, 2015[47]). In some countries, the development of communal and institutionalised dwellings for the elderly is on the rise, and their further development could be facilitated by changes to zoning and local planning regulations. Finally, it will be very important to coordinate housing with other key policy domains for the elderly, particularly health services, to ensure that the elderly can receive the long-term care supports they need to stay in their homes for as long as possible (OECD/EU, 2013[52]).

3.2.4. Invest in homelessness prevention and provide targeted support to the homeless

To effectively tackle homelessness, governments should invest in homeless prevention and provide targeted support to people who have become homeless. These strategies should be complemented by efforts to improve data collection efforts to better understand the extent and needs of the challenge.

Homeless prevention encompasses a broad range of housing support measures for low-income and vulnerable households that have been discussed in this report which, even if it is not the explicit aim, can help to prevent homelessness. Such support may be in the form of housing allowances (as in the vast majority of OECD countries), social (subsidised) housing, or mortgage relief for homeowners in financial distress. In addition, broader efforts to boost the supply of affordable housing or curb rising housing prices can prevent a higher incidence of homelessness; for instance, Norway's successful efforts to reduce homelessness have been part of a broader strategy to increase the affordable housing supply (OECD, 2020[53]).

More should be done to prevent homelessness by identifying at-risk populations and intervening *before* people become homeless. Australian researchers, for instance, developed a "risk of homelessness index", which captures a series of pathways to homelessness, such as a financial shock or job loss; a family breakdown; mental health issues or substance abuse, among other factors. The index was then mapped to identify geographic areas with a large share of people at risk of becoming homeless (Souza, Tanton and Abello, 2013[54]). Support to at-risk populations can take the form of temporary financial assistance, legal support, or mediation services for landlords and tenants. In the United States, for instance, comprehensive homelessness prevention programmes have been effective in reducing the number of people who enter homeless shelters; temporary financial assistance can reduce the average time spent in homeless shelters; and legal assistance to households facing eviction can also improve housing outcomes for renters (Evans, Phillips and Ruffini, 2019[55]). Scottish research shows that there is a spike in the use of health services *before* people are assessed as homeless, a sign that that the health system can play an important role in homeless prevention (Waugh, Rowley and Clarke, 2018[56]).

To help people who have become homeless return to stable housing, it is important that governments pursue tailored housing and social service solutions that respond to the increasing diversity of the homeless population, as well as the different drivers that lead to homelessness. For instance, people facing financial difficulties may only require temporary emergency housing support to help them get back on their feet. Meanwhile, homeless youth, veterans, migrants, women who are victims of domestic violence, or Indigenous populations may require additional social services beyond housing support, ranging from health care, counselling, childcare, language classes or labour market support. The type and level of support should be adapted to the needs of the diverse homeless population, as well as the specific needs of particular groups and local challenges. Evidence suggests that "Housing First" approaches, which provide immediate, permanent housing to the homeless, along with integrated service delivery, can be highly effective solutions for the chronically homeless, while emergency support, including rapid rehousing, can help the transitionally homeless (OECD, 2020[53]).

Effective solutions rely on good cooperation among national and local authorities, and non-governmental service providers. Countries that have reduced homelessness have often relied on a sustained political and strategic commitment by national government, working in close co-ordination with regional and local actors to develop tailored strategies. A number of countries, including Canada, Denmark, Finland, France and the United States, have adopted such an approach (OECD, 2020[53]). This is important to tackle effectively the very different homelessness challenges and populations that exist within countries. The Australian Government has bilateral agreements with state and territory governments under the National Housing and Homelessness Agreement (NHHA), which requires all state and territory governments to have a homelessness strategy that sets out reforms and initiatives that will contribute to a reduction in the incidence of homelessness. Co-operation across actors is essential, along with an ability to change often longstanding approaches and systems to homelessness. Involving the homeless in the design of strategies and policy responses can help policy makers better understand the specific needs and challenges of the population, as has been done in Canada's *Reaching Home* Homelessness Strategy.

Finally, homelessness is, by its very nature, a difficult circumstance to assess, as homeless individuals may be more or less "invisible" to public authorities and support institutions. There are significant methodological challenges in homelessness data collection in OECD countries that make it difficult to assess the full extent of homelessness. As a result, there is scope to improve data collection of homelessness and expand the methodological toolbox to better understand the challenges and needs of different homeless populations. Depending on the country, this could imply more regular data collection, investments in the integration of different data sources to better assess and support the homeless, along with efforts to expand the methodological toolbox to collect data. Innovative approaches to link administrative and survey data can provide a more comprehensive understanding of the challenges and needs of different homeless populations. For instance, researchers in Scotland (United Kingdom) linked homelessness and health datasets to find that at least 8% of the Scottish population in mid-2015 had experienced homelessness at some point in their lives – a much larger share than expected (Waugh et al., 2018[57]). The Australian government has bilateral agreements with all state and territory governments to work together to share and link datasets. In some cases, researchers are using big data to identify households at risk of homelessness, which could enable authorities to reach out *ex ante* to such households with prevention services. Canada has had success in systematising homelessness data through its homeless management information systems (for further detail, see (OECD, 2020[53])).

3.3. Addressing housing vulnerability to address housing vulnerability prompted by the COVID-19 pandemic

At the time of publishing this report, the COVID-19 crisis was continuing to unfold in countries and communities across the world. In addition to its economic, social and health impacts, the crisis has also brought to the fore many of the housing challenges discussed in this report. People living in overcrowded conditions – representing more than a quarter of all households in several OECD countries – have been unable to self-isolate effectively, putting themselves and their household at greater risk of contracting and spreading the disease. The confinement period has also posed challenges and risks to people living in poor quality housing, such as dwellings with a leaking roof or lacking basic sanitary facilities. The widespread shift of the workforce to teleworking is not feasible for households who do not have a computer or access to the Internet at home. In households with school-aged children, the digital divide risks deepening educational disparities during a period of extended school closures where many institutions have transitioned to distance learning.

Table 3.4. Many countries introduced emergency housing measures in response to COVID-19

Types of emergency, temporary housing measures introduced in OECD countries in response to COVID-19

Type of measure or support	Country
For tenants:	
Eviction ban due to missed payments	Australia*, Austria*, Belgium*, Canada*, France, Germany, Hungary, Ireland, Israel*, Luxembourg, the Netherlands, New Zealand, Portugal, Spain, United Kingdom, United States*
Deferment of rent payments	Austria, Mexico, Portugal*, Spain*
Temporary reduction or suspension of rent payments for some households	Australia*, Greece, Portugal*, Spain*
Rent freeze	Australia*, Ireland, New Zealand, Spain*
Reforms to financial support schemes for renters	Australia*, Japan*, Ireland, Luxembourg, Spain
For homeowners:	
Mortgage forbearance	Australia*, Austria, Belgium, Canada*, Colombia, the Czech Republic, Germany, Greece, Ireland, Israel, Italy, Lithuania, Mexico*, Portugal, the Slovak Republic, Spain, United Kingdom, United States*
Foreclosure ban due to missed payments	The Netherlands, United States*
For all households (regardless of tenure):	
Deferment of utility payments and/or assured continuity of service even if payment missed	Australia*, Austria, Belgium*, Colombia, Germany, Japan, Korea, Portugal*, Spain, United States*
Reforms to housing subsidy schemes	France (postponement of planned reform), Spain
For the homeless:	
Emergency support to provide shelter and/or services to the homeless	Australia, Austria, Canada, France, Ireland*, New Zealand, Portugal, Spain, United Kingdom, United States*

Note: List of measures as of 6 July 2020. * indicates that the measure applies only to some jurisdictions and/or to qualifying households.
Source: (OECD, 2020[24]) (OECD, 2020[23]) and the corresponding country tracker, http://oe.cd/covid19tablesocial.

At the same time, the COVID-19 crisis has also laid bare the affordability challenges of homeowners and renters across the OECD. Without assistance, workers who have been laid off or are temporarily unable to work may struggle to cover their monthly rent, mortgage or utilities payments. The homeless are acutely vulnerable to the spread of COVID-19 and lack the ability to effectively shelter in place. There is preliminary evidence in the United Kingdom and the United States suggesting that renters may be disproportionately affected by the crisis, because they are more likely than homeowners to be overburdened by housing costs (Chapter 2) and to work in the industries most affected by the pandemic (OECD, 2020[24]). There are concerns over a potential surge in evictions and, by extension, homelessness, once the temporary moratoria introduced by various governments are lifted, and especially in countries where economic activity has not yet fully resumed. In the United States, nearly 20% of renters reported that they failed to pay or deferred monthly rental payments in June 2020 (compared to 13% of homeowners with a mortgage); nearly a third of renters expressed no or only slight confidence that they would be able to pay the following month's rent (compared to 15% of homeowners with a mortgage) (United States Census Bureau, 2020[58]). More research will be needed to assess the impacts of the COVID-19 pandemic on housing outcomes across different groups and regions, as well as the extent to which lessons from the previous financial crisis remain relevant.

To address the immediate housing risks generated by the pandemic and the associated economic fallout, many government response packages to the crisis included temporary housing support measures, such as the suspension of evictions or foreclosures, the postponement of mortgage payments or reduction of rental payments, or emergency measures to support the homeless (Table 3.4). Such immediate (and in most cases, temporary) support has been essential to help vulnerable households cope during the crisis and maintain access to decent shelter. Some temporary support schemes may need to be extended in some cases, in some cases in order to support households that continue to struggle, and to avoid a sudden increase in evictions and homelessness. They should be phased out once conditions improve, in order to reduce potential negative long-term effects on the housing supply. Yet moving forward, governments will also need to develop longer-term, structural responses in order to overcome the persistent housing challenges and vulnerabilities facing households across the OECD.

References

Agence nationale pour la Rénovation Urbaine (ANRU) (2019), *Dossier spéciale : NPNRU Déjà 50 % des projets validés !*, Renouvellement le Mag n°13, https://www.anru.fr/fre/Mediatheque/Publications/Renouvellement-le-Mag-Le-magazine-participatif-du-renouvellement-urbain-n-13-avril-mai-2019 (accessed on 17 July 2019).   [34]

André, C. (2010), "A Bird's Eye View of OECD Housing Markets", *OECD Economics Department Working Papers*, No. 746, OECD Publishing, Paris, https://dx.doi.org/10.1787/5kmlh5qvz1s4-en.   [17]

Andrews, D. and A. Caldera Sánchez (2011), "The Evolution of Homeownership Rates in Selected OECD Countries: Demographic and Public Policy Influences", *OECD Journal: Economic Studies*, Vol. 1, https://www.oecd-ilibrary.org/docserver/eco_studies-2011-5kg0vswqpmg2.pdf?expires=1568809412&id=id&accname=ocid84004878&checksum=BD80B53B366EB54B6A4F571327AD1B20 (accessed on 18 September 2019).   [26]

Andrews, D. and A. Sánchez (2011), "The Evolution of Homeownership Rates in Selected OECD Countries: Demographic and Public Policy Influences", *OECD Journal: Economic Studies*, Vol. 2011, http://dx.doi.org/10.1787/19952856.   [16]

Arnott, R. (1995), "Time for Revisionism on Rent Control?", *Journal of Economic Perspectiv*, Vol. 9/1, pp. 99-120, https://pubs.aeaweb.org/doi/pdfplus/10.1257/jep.9.1.99 (accessed on 10 September 2019).   [41]

Berry, M. (2003), "Why is it important to boost the supply of affordable housing in Australia—and how can we do it?", *Urban Policy and Research*, Vol. 21/4, pp. 413-435, https://doi.org/10.1080/0811114032000147430.   [20]

Boffey, D. (2018), "Netherlands to build world's first habitable 3D printed houses | Art and design | The Guardian", https://www.theguardian.com/artanddesign/2018/jun/06/netherlands-to-build-worlds-first-habitable-3d-printed-houses (accessed on 4 December 2018). [14]

Brys, B. et al. (forthcoming), "Housing taxation policy, reconciling efficiency and equity objectives", *OECD Taxation Working Paper*. [22]

Brys, B. et al. (forthcoming), "Measuring effective taxation of housing: Building the foundations for policy reform", *OECD Taxation Working Paper*. [18]

Canada Mortgage Housing Corporation (CMHC) (2019), *Research Insight: Demand or Supply Side Housing Assistance? - Updating the debate*, https://eppdscrmssa01.blob.core.windows.net/cmhcprodcontainer/sf/project/cmhc/pubsandreports/research-insights/2019/research-insight-demand-supply-measures-pomeroy-69464-en.pdf?sv=2018-03-28&ss=b&srt=sco&sp=r&se=2021-05-07T03:55:04Z&st=2019-05-06T19:55:04 (accessed on 23 July 2019). [61]

Causa, O. and J. Pichelmann (forthcoming 2020), "Should I Stay or Should I Go? Housing and Residential Mobility across OECD Countries", *OECD Economics Department Working Papers*, http://dx.doi.org/ECO/CPE/WP1(2020)00. [33]

Causa, O. and N. Woloszko (2019), "Housing, wealth accumulation and wealth distribution: evidence and stylized facts", Economics Department - Economic Policy Committee, Working Party No. 1 on Macroeconomic and Structural Policy Analysis, http://dx.doi.org/ECO/CPE/WP1(2019)1. [21]

Chakrabarti, M. (2019), *These States Are Turning To Rent Control: How It Affects Affordable Housing*, Iowa Public Radio, https://www.iowapublicradio.org/post/these-states-are-turning-rent-control-how-it-affects-affordable-housing#stream/0 (accessed on 17 July 2019). [39]

Department for Communities and Local Government (2017), *Fixing our broken housing market*, http://www.gov.uk/government/publications (accessed on 23 July 2019). [63]

Dewilde, C. and P. De Decker (2016), "Changing Inequalities in Housing Outcomes across Western Europe, Housing", *Theory and Society*, Vol. 33/2, pp. 121-161, http://dx.doi.org/10.1080/14036096.2015.1109545. [2]

Diamond, R., T. Mcquade and F. Qian (2019), *The Effects of Rent Control Expansion on Tenants, Landlords, and Inequality: Evidence from San Francisco*, https://web.stanford.edu/~diamondr/DMQ.pdf (accessed on 15 July 2019). [38]

Dougherty, C. (2018), *Why Rent Control Is a Lightning Rod*, The New York Times, https://www.nytimes.com/2018/10/12/business/economy/rent-control-explained.html (accessed on 17 July 2019). [40]

EUROSTAT (2011), *Manual on sources and methods for the compilation of COFOG Statistics: Classification of the Functions of Government (COFOG)*, Eurostat, http://dx.doi.org/10.2785/16355. [70]

Evans, W., D. Phillips and K. Ruffini (2019), *Reducing and Preventing Homelessness: A Review of the Evidence and Charting a Research Agenda 1 A Report Prepared for the Abdul Latif Jameel Poverty Action Lab*. [55]

Fatica, S. and D. Prammer (2018), "Housing and the Tax System: How Large Are the Distortions in the Euro Area?", *Fiscal Studies*, Vol. 39/2, pp. 299-342, http://dx.doi.org/10.1111/1475-5890.12159. [67]

Favilukis, J., P. Mabille and N. Stern Stijn Van Nieuwerburgh (2018), *Affordable Housing and City Welfare **, https://sites.google.com/site/jackfavilukis.http://www.stern.nyu.edu/~svnieuwe. (accessed on 15 July 2019). [42]

Freddie Mac (2018), *The Major Challenge of Inadequate U.S. Housing Supply*, Economic & Housing Research Insight, http://www.freddiemac.com (accessed on 22 July 2019). [66]

Glaeser, E. and J. Gyourko (2003), "The Impact of Building Restrictions on Housing Affordability", *Federal Reserve Bank of New York Economic Policy Review* June 2003, https://www.newyorkfed.org/medialibrary/media/research/epr/03v09n2/0306glae.pdf (accessed on 15 July 2019). [12]

Glaeser, E. and J. Gyourko (2002), *The Impact of Zoning on Housing Affordability*, http://www.nber.org/papers/w8835 (accessed on 15 July 2019). [11]

Glaeser, E., J. Gyourko and R. Saks (2005), "Why Have Housing Prices Gone Up?", *American Economic Review Papers and Proceedings*, Vol. 95/2, pp. 329–333, https://inequality.stanford.edu/sites/default/files/media/_media/pdf/Reference%20Media/Glaeser_Gyourko_Saks_2005.pdf (accessed on 15 July 2019). [13]

Gromis, A. (2019), *Eviction: Intersection of Poverty, Inequality, and Housing*, https://www.un.org/development/desa/dspd/wp-content/uploads/sites/22/2019/05/GROMIS_Ashley_Paper.pdf. [36]

Gruber, J., A. Jensen and H. Kleven (2017), "Do People Respond to the Mortgage Interest Deduction? Quasi-experimental Evidence from Denmark", *NBER Working Paper Series*, National Bureau of Economic Research, https://www.nber.org/papers/w23600.pdf (accessed on 10 September 2019). [27]

Gurran, N. et al. (2018), *Inquiry into increasing affordable housing supply: Evidence-based principles and strategies for Australian policy and practice*, Australian Housing and Urban Research Institute (AHURI), http://dx.doi.org/10.18408/ahuri-7313001. [60]

Jenkins, B. (2009), "Rent Control: Do Economists Agree?", *Econ Journal Watch*, Vol. 6/1, pp. 73-112, https://econjwatch.org/File+download/238/2009-01-jenkins-reach_concl.pdf?mimetype=pdf (accessed on 17 September 2019). [45]

Knipp, K. (2019), *German cities struggle to curb housing shortage*, DW, https://www.dw.com/en/german-cities-struggle-to-curb-housing-shortage/a-49705919 (accessed on 23 July 2019). [64]

Lind, H. (2001), "Rent regulation: A conceptual and comparative analysis", *European Journal of Housing Policy*, Vol. 1/1, http://dx.doi.org/10.1080/14616710110036436. [37]

National Audit Office (2019), *Help to Buy: Equity Loan scheme - progress review*, National Audit Office, https://www.nao.org.uk/wp-content/uploads/2019/06/Help-to-Buy-Equity-Loan-scheme-progress-review.pdf (accessed on 8 July 2019). [68]

National Housing Supply Council (2012), *Housing Supply Responses to Change in Affordability*, https://www.treasury.gov.au/sites/default/files/2019-03/housing_supply_responses.pdf (accessed on 22 July 2019). [59]

OECD (2020), *Better data and policies to fight homelessness in the OECD. Policy Brief on Affordable Housing*, OECD Publishing, Paris, http://oe.cd/homelessness-2020. (accessed on 16 March 2020). [53]

OECD (2020), *OECD Employment Outlook 2020: Worker Security and the COVID-19 Crisis*, OECD Publishing, Paris, https://dx.doi.org/10.1787/1686c758-en. [24]

OECD (2020), *Policy Actions for Affordable Housing in Latvia*, http://www.oecd.org/economy/latvia-economic-snapshot/ (accessed on 2 July 2020). [10]

OECD (2020), *Social housing: A key part of past and future housing policy*. [25]

OECD (2020), *Supporting people and companies to deal with the COVID-19 virus: Options for an immediate employment and social-policy response*, OECD, Paris, http://oe.cd/covid19briefsocial (accessed on 14 April 2020). [23]

OECD (2019), *Affordable Housing Database - OECD*, http://www.oecd.org/social/affordable-housing-database.htm (accessed on 4 December 2018). [9]

OECD (2019), *OECD Affordable Housing Database*, http://www.oecd.org/social/affordable-housing-database/. [3]

OECD (2019), *OECD Economic Surveys: Luxembourg*, https://www.oecd-ilibrary.org/docserver/424839c1-en.pdf?expires=1563834462&id=id&accname=ocid84004878&checksum=23D9DF3D693C886FB8B08362CA9BB6A5 (accessed on 23 July 2019). [65]

OECD (2018), *Opportunities for All: OECD Framework for Policy Action on Inclusive Growth*, https://www.oecd-ilibrary.org/docserver/9789264301665-en.pdf?expires=1559813226&id=id&accname=ocid84004878&checksum=FB84F54E2BA978AD3170920AA4FBD722 (accessed on 6 June 2019). [1]

OECD (2018), *Taxation of household savings*, OECD Publishing, Paris, http://dx.doi.org/doi.org/10.1787/19900538. [19]

OECD (2017), *The Governance of Land Use in OECD Countries: Policy Analysis and Recommendations*, OECD Publishing, Paris, https://dx.doi.org/10.1787/9789264268609-en. [4]

OECD (2015), *Ageing in Cities*, OECD Publishing, Paris, https://dx.doi.org/10.1787/9789264231160-en. [47]

OECD (2015), *OECD Territorial Reviews: Valle de Mexico*, https://www.oecd-ilibrary.org/docserver/9789264245174-en.pdf?expires=1563201034&id=id&accname=ocid84004878&checksum=AC8810901EAA9580B7A83E47DAEC19A2 (accessed on 15 July 2019). [6]

OECD (2015), *OECD Urban Policy Reviews: Mexico 2015: Transforming Urban Policy and Housing Finance*, OECD Urban Policy Reviews, OECD Publishing, Paris, https://dx.doi.org/10.1787/9789264227293-en. [7]

OECD (2011), *Economic Policy Reforms 2011: Going for Growth*, OECD Publishing, Paris, https://dx.doi.org/10.1787/growth-2011-en. [28]

OECD (1998), *The Battle against Exclusion: Social Assistance in Belgium, the Czech Republic, the Netherlands and Norway*, OECD Publishing, Paris, https://dx.doi.org/10.1787/9789264012035-en. [46]

OECD (forthcoming), *Social housing: A key part of past and future housing policy*. [8]

OECD/EU (2013), *A Good Life in Old Age?: Monitoring and Improving Quality in Long-term Care*, OECD Health Policy Studies, OECD Publishing, Paris, https://dx.doi.org/10.1787/9789264194564-en. [52]

Oswald, A. (2009), "The Housing Market and Europe's Unemployment: A Non-technical Paper*", in *Homeownership and the Labour Market in Europe*, Oxford University Press, http://dx.doi.org/10.1093/acprof:oso/9780199543946.003.0003. [31]

Oswald, A. (1996), "A Conjecture on the Explanation for High Unemployment in the Industrialized Nations: Part I", *University of Warwick Economic Research Paper* 475, http://wrap.warwick.ac.uk/1664/1/WRAP_Oswald_475_twerp_475.pdf (accessed on 12 September 2019). [32]

Peaker, G. (2013), *The hidden dangers of shared ownership | Housing Network | The Guardian*, The Guardian, https://www.theguardian.com/housing-network/2013/sep/03/hidden-dangers-shared-ownership (accessed on 17 July 2019). [49]

Phillips, L. (2020), *Decentralisation and Governance in the Housing Sector*, OECD WORKING PAPERS ON FISCAL FEDERALISM, https://www.oecd-ilibrary.org/docserver/2d3c3241-en.pdf?expires=1593432474&id=id&accname=guest&checksum=BCC18E67833895799AE01EBB7344AD3F (accessed on 29 June 2020). [5]

Salvi del Pero, A. et al. (2016), "Policies to promote access to good-quality affordable housing in OECD countries", *OECD Social, Employment and Migration Working Papers*, No. 176, OECD Publishing, Paris, https://dx.doi.org/10.1787/5jm3p5gl4djd-en. [15]

Sánchez, A. and D. Andrews (2011), "Residential Mobility and Public Policy in OECD Countries", *OECD Journal: Economic Studies*, Vol. 2011/11, http://dx.doi.org/10.1787/19952856. [29]

Sánchez, A. and D. Andrews (2011), "To Move or not to Move: What Drives Residential Mobility Rates in the OECD?", *OECD Economics Department Working Papers*, No. 846, http://dx.doi.org/ttps://doi.org/10.1787/18151973. [30]

Slaug, B. et al. (2017), "Improved Housing Accessibility for Older People in Sweden and Germany: Short Term Costs and Long-Term Gains", *International Journal of Environmental Research and Public Health*, Vol. 14/964, http://dx.doi.org/10.3390/ijerph14090964. [51]

Souza, G., R. Tanton and A. Abello (2013), *Geographical Analysis of the Risk of Homelessness*, http://www.canberra.edu.au/centres/natsem/ (accessed on 28 October 2019). [54]

Stichting Perspectiefverklaring (n.d.), *Stichting Perspectiefverklaring*, 2019, https://www.perspectiefverklaring.nl/ (accessed on 15 July 2019). [50]

Tax Policy Center (2016), *Tax Benefit of the Deductions for Home Mortgage Interest and Property Tax by Expanded Cash Income Percentile, 2016*, Tax Policy Center - Urban Institute and Brookings Institution, https://www.taxpolicycenter.org/model-estimates/individual-income-tax-expenditures-july-2016/t16-0165-tax-benefit-deductions-home (accessed on 8 July 2019). [69]

Terner Center for Housing Innovation, U. (2018), *Finding Common Ground on Rent Control A Terner Center Policy Brief*, http://ternercenter.berkeley.edu/uploads/Rent_Control_Paper_053018.pdf (accessed on 15 July 2019). [43]

United States Census Bureau (2020), *Household Pulse Survey Data Tables*, https://www.census.gov/programs-surveys/household-pulse-survey/data.html (accessed on 20 July 2020). [58]

Wang, R. et al. (2019), "Tracking Growth and Evaluating Performance of Shared Equity Homeownership Programs During Housing Market Fluctuations", No. Working Paper WP19RW1, Lincoln Institute of Land Policy, https://www.lincolninst.edu/sites/default/files/pubfiles/wang_wp19rw1_rev_0.pdf (accessed on 11 July 2019). [48]

Waugh, A. et al. (2018), "Health and Homelessness in Scotland: Research". [57]

Waugh, A., D. Rowley and A. Clarke (2018), "The relationship between health and homelessness in Scotland". [56]

Whitehead, C. and P. Williams (2018), *Assessing the evidence on Rent Control from an International Perspective*, LSE London, https://research.rla.org.uk/wp-content/uploads/LSE-International-Evidence-on-Rent-Control-Report-2018-Final.pdf (accessed on 17 September 2019). [35]

Wilson, W. (2019), *Stimulating Housing Supply - Government Initiatives (England)*, House of Commons Library. [62]

World Bank (2018), *Living and Leaving: Housing, Mobility and Welfare in the European Union*, https://www.worldbank.org/en/region/eca/publication/living-and-leaving (accessed on 15 July 2019). [44]

Notes

1 It is not possible to distinguish between different types of housing investment data, e.g. higher-end luxury housing and/or social or affordable housing. The data here are an indication of investment in all types of housing.

2 Public capital transfers for housing development (COFOG series D9CG) refers to indirect capital expenditure made through transfers to organisations outside of government. Housing development includes, among other things, the acquisition of land needed for the construction of dwellings, the construction or purchase and remodelling of dwelling units for the general public or for people with special

needs, and grants or loans to support the expansion, improvement or maintenance of the housing stock. See (EUROSTAT, 2011[70]) for more detail.

3 For instance, in Australia, "supply has generally failed to meet demand" (National Housing Supply Council, 2012[59]), and the country's affordable housing deficit was estimated at 20 000 dwellings in 2018 (Gurran et al., 2018[60]). Canada estimates that 1.3 million urban households living in metropolitan areas were "in core housing need"3 in 2017, with particular shortages in the affordable housing and rental housing supply (Canada Mortgage Housing Corporation (CMHC), 2019[61]). England faces "a crisis in housing supply" (Wilson, 2019[62]): an average of 160 000 dwellings have been built yearly since the 1970s, with more than 225 000 now needed each year to satisfy population growth and address decades of under-supply (Department for Communities and Local Government, 2017[63]). In Germany, cities in particular struggle to address the housing shortage (Knipp, 2019[64]).

Luxembourg also suffers from an imbalance between supply and demand (OECD, 2019[65]). In the United States, there has been a "large and persistent shortfall" in the housing stock in recent years (Freddie Mac, 2018[66]).

4 For instance, a National Audit Office report found that the UK's "Help to Buy" scheme – which has provided over 200 000 equity loans aiming to increase home ownership and boost housing supply – resulted in three-fifths of the scheme's beneficiaries could have bought a property (but not necessarily the same house) without "Help to Buy". One-third could have bought the house they wanted without the scheme (National Audit Office, 2019[68]). By extension, mortgage interest deductibility measures tend to be regressive (Andrews and Sánchez, 2011[16]; Fatica and Prammer, 2018[67]). A 2016 assessment of the tax relief measures for homeowners in the United States found that such support mostly benefited high-income taxpayers (Tax Policy Center, 2016[69]). Evidence from Denmark assessing the impacts on housing outcomes for different income groups that resulted from major tax reforms in the 1980s, which sharply reduced the mortgage deduction for high-income taxpayers, found that: i) tax subsidies to promote home ownership had a "tightly estimated and robust zero effect" on whether households chose to rent or own; ii) tax subsidies were clearly shown to influence the size and value of the homes purchased, with a decrease in the tax subsidy resulting to important reductions in housing size and appraised values; and iii) the largest effect of tax subsidies was on household financial (rather than housing) decisions (Gruber, Jensen and Kleven, 2017[27]).

Annex A. Household consumption expenditure and measurement data

Household consumption expenditure measurement and data

Building on the work prepared for OECD (2019[1]), some of the analysis in this report draws on micro-data relating to household consumption expenditures, which come from household budget surveys. The expenditure categories available in national surveys have been harmonised by the OECD in accordance with the Classification of Individual Consumption according to Purpose (COICOP) (UN Department of Economic and Social Affairs - Statistics Division, 2018[2]). This classification, developed by the United Nations Statistics Division, divides consumption into categories, with 12 main categories for the household sector. Data used follows the COICOP classification, with the exception of "insurance related to health", classified as part of "health" consumption instead of "miscellaneous goods and services".

Some categories have been combined with others. For instance, the sum of "Recreation and culture", "restaurants and hotels" and "alcoholic beverages, tobacco and narcotics" are referred to as "leisure". The sum of "food and non-alcoholic beverages" and "clothing and footwear" are referred to as "food and clothing". The sum of "furnishings, household equipment and routine household maintenance" and "Miscellaneous goods and services" (excluding "insurance related to health") are referred to as "other".

Data were collected for 28 OECD countries (data are not available for Australia, Canada, Iceland, Israel, Japan, Korea, New Zealand and Switzerland). Data for EU countries and Chile were readily compatible with COICOP. Data for the United States and Mexico were reclassified in accordance with COICOP. Data for EU countries for 1998, 2005 and 2015 were imputed with growth rates by quintile of disposable income based on data published by Eurostat (except for France, the United Kingdom and Spain between 2006-15). Incomes have been adjusted for non-reporting using experimental statistics on income published by Eurostat (Eurostat, n.d.[3]).

For a full explanation of the data and data sources, please refer to Box 4.2 and Annex 4.A in OECD (2019[1]).

Annex B. Housing overburden rates, by age

Table B.1. Housing overburden rates, by age

Share of population (who do not live in dwellings that are owned outright) spending more than 40% of disposable income on mortgage and rent, by age, in percent, 2017 or last year available

	15 to 29 years	30 to 49 years	50 to 64 years	65 or more years	Below 15
Australia	10%	10%	12%	19%	9%
Austria	10%	7%	4%	6%	6%
Belgium	8%	9%	12%	21%	7%
Chile	16%	14%	14%	22%	16%
Denmark	28%	14%	8%	17%	12%
Finland	13%	6%	9%	14%	5%
France	9%	5%	7%	5%	3%
Germany	6%	4%	6%	7%	
Greece	28%	22%	24%	20%	20%
Hungary	11%	10%	13%	16%	9%
Iceland	27%	18%	20%	11%	15%
Ireland	11%	7%	10%	9%	6%
Italy	11%	12%	13%	14%	10%
Japan		12%	13%	20%	
Korea	6%	2%	4%	11%	
Latvia	4%	3%	6%	3%	3%
Luxembourg	18%	19%	19%	16%	17%
Netherlands	11%	7%	7%	9%	5%
Norway	20%	7%	5%	5%	5%
Poland	13%	6%	5%	6%	6%
Portugal	12%	9%	11%	7%	8%
Slovenia	6%	5%	5%	6%	4%
Spain	17%	14%	18%	13%	16%
Sweden	15%	8%	9%	20%	7%
Switzerland	5%	5%	7%	14%	5%
United Kingdom	11%	10%	13%	18%	11%
United States	16%	12%	13%	20%	17%

Note: The data exclude households living in dwellings that are owned outright.
Source: OECD calculations based on European Union Statistics on Income and Living Conditions (EU SILC) survey 2018 except for Ireland, the Slovak Republic, and the United Kingdom (2017), and Iceland (2016); the Household, Income and Labour Dynamics Survey (HILDA) for Australia (2017); Encuesta de Caracterización Socioeconómica Nacional (CASEN) for Chile (2017); the Korean Housing Survey (2017); Encuesta Nacional de Ingresos y Gastos de los Hogares (ENIGH) for Mexico (2016); American Community Survey (ACS) for the United States (2016).

Annex C. Trends in overall investment in housing

Direct investment (gross fixed capital formation) in housing grew significantly in most countries prior to the financial crisis, before dropping sharply around 2007 and then increasing steadily from around 2013. However, trends vary considerably across countries (Table C.1):

- A number of countries experienced considerable volatility in housing investment during the years around the crisis, but have since recovered to surpass pre-crisis investment levels (e.g. Australia, Belgium, Estonia, Iceland, Korea, Lithuania, the Netherlands, New Zealand, Norway, Sweden and Switzerland).

- Meanwhile, housing investment has steadily increased since 2000 in Canada, Chile, the Czech Republic, Finland, Israel, Luxembourg.

- Housing investment has yet to fully recover from the Great Recession in Hungary, Ireland, Italy, Spain, the United States, the United Kingdom and, in particular, Greece.

- Relative to 2000, Latvia, Portugal and Slovenia have experienced a drop in overall housing investment.

- Housing investment levels have remained relatively stable in Austria and Germany since 2000, nonetheless declining somewhat in the 2000s.

Table C.1. Overall investment in housing, 2000-19

Gross fixed capital formation, housing, volume, Index 2000=100

	2000	2005	2010	2015	2019
Australia	100	123	120	141	143
Austria	100	89	88	90	104
Belgium	100	115	113	112	124
Canada	100	149	152	172	175
Chile	100	129	122	139	138
Czech Republic	100	115	163	196	237
Denmark	100	137	87	99	126
Estonia	100	364	209	381	579
Finland	100	117	121	116	139
France	100	116	107	101	115
Germany	100	80	81	94	107
Greece	100	122	74	9	10
Hungary	100	153	105	84	127
Iceland	100	167	63	87	218
Ireland	100	161	53	36	74
Israel	100	94	123	163	184
Italy	100	117	109	79	87
Japan	100	93	63	70	73
Korea	100	155	113	169	203
Latvia	100	103	58	78	70
Lithuania	100	170	192	298	345

	2000	2005	2010	2015	2019
Luxembourg	100	106	135	215	219
Netherlands	100	103	83	78	117
New Zealand	100	128	92	147	175
Norway	100	140	123	171	185
Poland	100	113	139	143	131
Portugal	100	77	46	32	42
Slovak Republic	100	86	85	88	131
Slovenia	100	114	102	68	82
Spain	100	135	92	75	101
Sweden	100	158	155	204	215
Switzerland	100	114	110	124	124
United Kingdom	100	125	92	107	111
United States	100	134	58	84	90
OECD average	100	129	107	125	150

Source: OECD Economic Outlook No 106 (Edition 2019/2).

References

Eurostat (n.d.), *Experimental Statistics - Overview*, 2019, https://ec.europa.eu/eurostat/web/experimental-statistics/ (accessed on 15 July 2019).   [3]

OECD (2019), *Under Pressure: The Squeezed Middle Class*, OECD Publishing, Paris, https://dx.doi.org/10.1787/689afed1-en.   [1]

UN Department of Economic and Social Affairs - Statistics Division (2018), *Classification of Individual Consumption According to Purpose (COICOP) 2018*, United Nations, https://unstats.un.org/unsd/classifications/business-trade/desc/COICOP_english/COICOP_2018_-_pre-edited_white_cover_version_-_2018-12-26.pdf (accessed on 15 July 2019).   [2]

www.ingramcontent.com/pod-product-compliance
Lightning Source LLC
Chambersburg PA
CBHW080620270326
41928CB00016B/3143